THE PROPER CHARLIE

TO RICHARD
2ND BEST BARMAN BEHIND
NORMAN
BEST WISHES STEVEN

THE PROPER CHARLIE

MY AUTOBIOGRAPHY

CHARLIE MILLER

WITH SCOTT McDERMOTT

BLACK & WHITE PUBLISHING

First published 2014
by Black & White Publishing Ltd
29 Ocean Drive, Edinburgh EH6 6JL

1 3 5 7 9 10 8 6 4 2   14 15 16 17

ISBN: 978 1 84502 827 5

The publisher has made every reasonable effort to contact copyright
holders of images in this book. Any errors are inadvertent and
anyone who for any reason has not been contacted is invited to write to
the publisher so that a full acknowledgment can be made in subsequent
editions of this work.

A CIP catalogue record for this book is available from the British Library.

Typeset by Iolaire Typesetting, Newtonmore
Printed and bound by Gutenberg Press, Malta

This is for my uncles, Benny and Jim, for all the help and advice they've given me over the years. For Jeannie and Jimmy Bird, Lenny and Ricky, RIP. For my mother-in-law, Margaret, and my ma, who won't let cancer beat them. For Caroline, Demi and Jordan, who mean everything to me. And for my wee gran, who is sorely missed.

Charlie Miller

For Debbie and Grace, whose love and support has been invaluable. And for Harry, who will always be in our thoughts.

Scott McDermott

Co-author Scott McDermott is the *Sunday Mail*'s chief sports writer. Born in Glasgow, he grew up in Castlemilk, the same housing estate as Charlie Miller. After failing to make it as a footballer at Dundee and Partick Thistle, he gained an Honours Degree in Media Studies in 2002. He became a full-time sports journalist at the *Sunday Mail* in 2003 and since then has covered matches at Premiership, Champions League and international level. He has also reported at major sporting events like the Open and Wimbledon. Scott lives in Glasgow with his wife Debbie and daughter Grace.

FOREWORD
BY ALLY McCOIST

JUST the mention of Charlie Miller's name makes me smile. What a lad he is, a great boy. I'll never forget the first day he walked into the Rangers dressing-room at sixteen. I thought, 'Who's this cheeky wee so-and-so?'

He was absolutely fearless as a kid. Charlie was never going to win any shyness awards, that's for sure. From the minute he joined us, he was right into the dressing-room banter. Man alive, he was in it head first. He was giving full-time, established pros like myself stick from the off. It was unbelievable. He didn't even give himself a settling-in period. We all got it: myself, Ian Durrant, Mark Hateley, Andy Goram, Richard Gough – and we'd all been there for years. But – BANG! He was right at it.

We used to have a wee battle of the banter. Charlie was part of the young team with the likes of Craig Moore and Derek McInnes. But he was the leader of that gang. And he could play, by the way. The thing I always remember is that he was brilliant at allowing the ball to run through him all in one movement. He also had great vision and could score a goal. But, boy, he should have done better with the talent he had.

If I was going to be critical, he should have achieved a lot more as a footballer – because Charlie Miller is the second most gifted youngster I've ever seen, behind Durrant. Only Charlie will know whether he has regrets about his career. He didn't do badly, winning four league titles, a League Cup and being part of nine-in-a-row at Rangers. In my opinion, however, he could and should have won more.

People will automatically assume that Paul Gascoigne's influence had a lot to do with that. But Gazza was good and bad for Charlie. That's the truth. He was brilliant for him in the sense that he was a top-class player. Charlie looked up to Gazza, and rightly so – he was one of the best players any of us ever played with. And Charlie got close to him off the pitch. He and Gazza were thick as thieves. But, being younger, Charlie found it difficult to distance himself from the madness of Gazza. He got himself too involved. The rest of us all loved Paul. We appreciated the brilliance and understood the madness that surrounded him. The difference was, we were capable of taking a step back from it at the appropriate times. But, to Charlie's detriment, he was right bang in the middle of it. That's not a criticism of Charlie or Paul; it's just an opinion. The pair of them were great together, both on and off the pitch, but Charlie has never quite managed to shift the 'Jack the Lad' persona and I think that has overshadowed his ability at times.

He was a sensational young player and his natural talent was phenomenal. The fact that Walter Smith threw him into the Rangers side at seventeen years of age tells you everything. Walter *never* did that. But he did it with Charlie because he knew he was good enough to handle it. The old yin wasn't one to pitch you in unless he was 100 per cent confident in you. Charlie is the only one Walter ever did that with. So that's how good he was as a youngster coming through at Ibrox.

He walked into a training session with Brian Laudrup, Gough, Hateley and Durrant, and held his own. Even back then, Charlie didn't look out of place. He was just a terrific footballer. I've never seen a kid before or since who has been as good at seeing the whole picture in front of him. His peripheral vision on the pitch was incredible.

Youngsters come in and they have different qualities. But I can honestly say, Charlie had the whole lot. I fully expected Charlie Miller, at the very worst, to be a stalwart in the Rangers team for the best part of a decade, because he had the ability to do so. He could also have played at the highest level in England. It's a travesty that he only picked up one Scotland cap and everyone would agree, with his quality, that he should have got more.

What I like about him, though, is that he went to different countries and played. He was all over the place: in England, Norway, Belgium and Australia. There was nowhere he wouldn't go in search of a game of football, as he tried to further his career. For doing that, I'll always have enormous respect for him.

I actually love Charlie, I really do. And I love the fact that he's now coaching kids. Not only is it great for these youngsters, it's brilliant for Charlie as well, because it gives him responsibility. It gives him an opportunity to put something back into football. He's well qualified to teach them the errors of his ways. He can coach them and try to make them more talented. But he can also speak to them, because Charlie has had an unbelievable footballing life. He's played all over the world, with and against some of the best players around. He has a wealth of experience and it would be a tragedy if he wasn't allowed to pass that on to a younger generation.

Having spoken to him when he was at Murray Park recently, I think he's enjoying that responsibility. And one of Charlie's best qualities, if not the best, is that he hasn't changed one bit. He's still the same boy who bounced into that dressing-room twenty years ago. Honestly, he's in here two minutes now, and he's taking the mickey out of me again. And that's why I love him. He's got the most wicked sense of humour I've ever came across.

But he's also very kind. That's where Charlie and Gazza are very similar. There are many similarities between them. They don't have a single bad bone in their bodies. They have one or two daft ones, but no bad ones. Charlie is incredibly loyal and true to himself in that he's never forgotten his roots or where he came from. He'll never abandon his pals. Maybe that kind of loyalty has gone against him in his career and in his life. But is it a crime? I don't think so.

CONTENTS

PROLOGUE

HAMPDEN PARK. I'm eighteen years of age and celebrating my first Old Firm victory in the Rangers dressing-room. We've just beaten Celtic 3–1 and the boys are ecstatic. The gaffer, Walter Smith, is delighted. I've teed up Mark Hateley to score the second goal of his double, with Brian Laudrup getting the third after a typically mesmerising run.

I've played really well, I know I have.

I'm looking around the dressing-room, at guys like Andy Goram and Stuart McCall, and I'm thinking, 'Fuck, it doesn't get any better than this.' It was the day I realised I could play in that company. After that, I knew I could mix it with the best in Scotland.

Guys like Paul McStay and John Collins were playing for Celtic. I belonged in that company, even at eighteen. I didn't look out of place alongside the likes of Hateley and Laudrup in a Rangers jersey. There's a cracking picture of me on top of Mark's shoulders in front of the fans. It was in all the papers the next day. I was as high as a kite afterwards, so happy. What a brilliant feeling it was. I knew the significance of beating Celtic. As if I didn't know already, Walter had drummed it into me beforehand. So had the players. It was a huge result, in terms of us going on to win the title that year.

There was no way we could lose against them.

1

At that point I felt like I could do no wrong. I was being tipped as Scotland's hottest property and the best young talent in the country.

It was 30 October 1994. I had made it.

1

FAMILY

18 MARCH 1976: I was born in Glasgow's Rottenrow Hospital, Charles Miller.

My ma, as I call her, Christine Miller, was on her own for the birth. And to this day I don't know who my father is.

I've never wanted to know and I have no desire to find out in the future. People might find that hard to believe. But not once has it crossed my mind to seek out my dad and he probably still doesn't even know I'm his son.

My ma had me when she was just eighteen years old. She was young and living in Castlemilk, one of Glasgow's roughest housing estates, and it must have been tough for her. The prospect of trying to bring me up on her own must have been a scary thought for someone who was only a teenager herself.

I've never asked her about who my dad is. Even now, I'm not interested. I wouldn't want to put my ma in an awkward position. If he knew, I'm pretty sure he'd have come out of the woodwork when I eventually went on to play for Rangers and was in the public eye. But no one has ever tried to contact me or get in touch. I have no regrets over that and it's something that has never bothered me. I can say that honestly. He could be anybody. He could be out there now, but he could be a horrible person who isn't worth knowing anyway. I don't know. When so many years pass by, you care about it a lot less and I can't envisage a moment where I feel the need to ask my ma who he was, where he came from or what he was like.

My ma has obviously never felt the need – or wanted – to tell me who he was. I don't blame or resent her for that; it's her choice. And I'd never want to make her feel uncomfortable by asking about him. That's just not me.

I wouldn't say it's a taboo subject, because it has never been on the agenda. I certainly haven't suffered from not knowing, and if I go through my whole life without him in it, I won't be any worse off.

Most footballers talk about their dads in glowing terms. About how they were the biggest influence on their careers, especially growing up. That's certainly not the case for me. People ask me if I missed out on having a dad, but I didn't. Not at all. Luckily, I had my ma's two brothers, Uncle Benny and Uncle Jim, and they were huge 'father figures' for me as a kid. I didn't miss out on anything my real dad could have given me – Benny and Jim saw to that. If I hadn't had those two, I definitely wouldn't have made it as a footballer. I would never have got anywhere, for a start. Those two got me into football at a young age and took me all over Britain to play and train.

My ma was naive and immature, and having a child obviously took its toll on her. That's why, from as early as I can remember, I lived with my gran, Isa Miller, my ma's ma. I don't even remember the point where my ma said she was sending me to live with my gran. I was just always there. As a kid, when I was at my ma's house, I vividly recall running away because I wanted to go back to stay at my gran's. That's where I was happiest.

I have nothing against my ma for what she did. She was young and it was her first baby. She probably thought she couldn't cope. I think she was still, let's just say, 'living her life' a bit at that stage as well, so going to live at my gran's was probably the best option for all of us.

My relationship with my ma is fine now. We get on well, except when she's moaning at me. Seriously, I've never had any resentment against her. As I got older, I'm sure she'd have taken me back at her place, but I didn't want to go. She could probably see how happy I was at my gran's.

I lived at 27 Stravanan Road in Castlemilk, in an old tenement close. I loved it. And the earliest memory I have is of playing football in the street. I swear we used to have good summers in Scotland. Well, we did when I was growing up.

Castlemilk is a housing scheme that was built in the 1950s to accommodate families from the city's slums, like the Gorbals. To this day, it's one of Scotland's largest estates, with around 15,000 people living there. It doesn't have a great reputation and it has problems with violence, youth disorder, alcohol and drug abuse. But no one can deny that there is still a great sense of community in Castlemilk – and it provided me with a terrific upbringing. It shaped me as a person.

There is a vision in my head of me kicking a ball around in the big corner garden on Stravanan Road, and we'd make our own goals with bits of wood. There was an old guy called Cha who lived in the bottom flat of that close. He'd help us with hammering the posts to the bar and we'd go and find nets from somewhere.

Cha would sit and watch us playing from his window. I know, in this day and age that might sound a bit weird, but he wasn't a bad guy at all, he just loved watching all the games and we'd play until eleven o'clock at night sometimes. It was great because my gran stayed right across the road and my ma and uncles Benny and Jim also lived close by, so it wasn't a problem.

My gran was something special. She was a unique wee woman. I loved her to bits and, having spent my entire childhood with her, I wouldn't change anything. It was heartbreaking when she died in 1998, when I was only twenty-two.

I always got lots of attention from my gran. I wasn't born with curly hair, but I ended up looking as if I had a perm because she would sit me on her knee and curl it on her finger. We spent a lot of time together, which is why is was so hard to lose her sixteen years ago.

She was brilliant, just a really nice woman. She smoked but would only ever take a couple of draws from a fag before putting the douts in a big tub. I remember guys from the street used to come in and steal all the douts. They'd run in and shout at me, 'Are there any of Isa's douts there?' Everyone in the area knew who she was.

I'll never forget the time she left the gas on and blew up the flat! Luckily, there was no one in there at the time. I was only about twelve. My gran's cockatoo even managed to survive the blast and it made the local newspapers, and I had mixed feelings about that!

Honestly, that bird was a pain in the arse. Before I knew she'd got it, I came in after school one day and this thing flew right at me. I immediately flew out the front door, screaming the place down. At that point, my gran and aunt Edith were walking in and I yelled at them, 'Don't go in, there's an *eagle* in the hoose!' But the bird stayed and my gran loved it – even though it used to shit all over the place.

After the explosion the place was a wreck, but the council just moved us from the top flat down to the bottom one in the same block. That's just the way it was back then.

My cousin, Shelley Miller, also lived with me, and her mum, Edith, stayed up the stairs in the same close. Edith was a lorry driver who was away a lot, so I think that's why Shelley ended up in with us.

In 1979, my ma had another baby and my sister Susan stayed with her. By then, my ma was a bit older and more mature than she had been when I was born. However, such was the allure of living with me and my gran, I think Susan would have loved to come over the road as well.

Sadly, Susan had next to no contact with her dad either, in a similar way to myself. Again, like me, Susan never suffered from

6

not having a father figure in her life. I suppose we just accepted that that's the way it was. We never once judged our ma or questioned why it was the case. To my knowledge, Susan has also never sought to find her dad and has no plans to do so.

Susan and I get on fine. She is three years younger than me and she's a good lassie. When she has a drink in her she can be a bit nuts, but her heart is in the right place. She's given me a niece, Charlie, and a nephew, Bobby, who I love to bits. They're really good kids and they're being brought up in Castlemilk, the same as me. My own son Jordan goes up and stays with them quite often and I get on well with Susan. She had a tough time as a kid growing up, but she's matured into a respectable woman.

Eight years after me, my little brother John was born to a different father again, but this time he played a big role in John's, Susan's and my own life. John McFaulds was a good man and we got on well. He was an important part of young John's upbringing, but sadly he passed away in 2008 after a heart attack.

My brother John is a decent boy and he's doing well for himself. He works at the Toryglen Regional Football Centre in Glasgow. John's a good lad and he's a worker. I would have probably liked to have a brother closer to me in age, but we get on great now. He's a big Rangers fan and we also play seven-a-sides together, even though he'll never be as good as his big brother!

Going to live with my gran was the best thing for me at the time. It wasn't that my ma 'moved me on'; she just felt it would be better for me and for her, which I totally understand now. I've never felt the need to quiz her on it, because she did the right thing by me. I had a good family around me when I was a kid and that's all that matters. We were all tight-knit and I've never seen it as a problem.

When I was growing up there was other extended family around too, like my auntie Josephine, who was just across the road in a bottom flat. She's now in America. And just along from her I had my auntie Janet and uncle Jimmy Copland, who later emigrated to Australia. So we were a close unit, all living in the same area.

I'm not going to lie. It wasn't an easy upbringing in Castlemilk. But I don't want any sympathy because I loved it and it was a great grounding for me. We never had much as a family, but, because of that, I never expected too much. There was always food in the house, and if I wanted a sweetie, I could always get one. I never went hungry, that's for sure.

My ma always worked. She had cleaning jobs and worked in the bookies at one point as well, so my childhood wasn't difficult, as such. It was just a tough, working-class part of Glasgow where you had to graft for everything. For example, I couldn't always get a pair of football boots when I needed them. I used to wear Dunlop Romas, which were eight pounds out of Shoefayre in Castlemilk Arcade. But it didn't make any difference to me how cheap my boots were because I was still the best player in my team.

During the summer holidays, I'd go away with a few mates from Stravanan and try to make money. We'd hunt for golf balls at Linn Park, then go over to Clarkston and get ourselves some cash for them. I never got into much bother when I was a young kid. My upbringing taught me a lot.

Growing up in Castlemilk, you can never think you're better than anyone. You'll get battered if you do: it's as simple as that. I was always wary of swanning around thinking I was the bee's knees, because people would start bad-mouthing me.

The main thing I knew when I was growing up was that family is important. And I found out all about that because I was just eighteen when I had a child of my own and it was a shock to my system. It was a pivotal moment in my life and I wasn't sure how I'd deal with being a father myself, which I'll go into later. But fatherhood is a wonderful thing and I wouldn't change anything for the world. I've been blessed with two brilliant kids, Demi and Jordan. Like any parent, I'd do anything for them, and we're really close.

My daughter Demi is a great lassie, and she was born on my gran's birthday, 14 May, which was special. Demi's nineteen now and is at college. She wants to be an actress and has already performed at the Pavilion Theatre in Glasgow. She loves to be on stage and express herself – a bit like me when I was on the football pitch. She knows what she wants and she's clever. If she's not like her dad – and does the right things in life – she'll achieve everything she wants. She's single-minded and intelligent, so the world's her oyster. Jordan will always be my boy, and he's a great lad. He's so laid-back at times he's almost horizontal. He'll be sixteen in December and, despite battling dyslexia, he's stuck in at school and is doing well. I'm really proud of him.

People asked if having a kid changed me because I was so young, but it didn't – because I was still a kid myself. I like to think I've been a good da, though, and I love them so much. They have a really good mum and a good family around them, especially on my wife Caroline's side.

Caroline was a hairdresser in the shopping arcade in Castlemilk when we first got together twenty-two years ago. We'd been at high school together and she was a year older than me. I can still remember the first time we ever kissed. She'd had a couple of drinks at the Oasis pub with her pals and I was coming out of the Castlemilk Community Centre. I met her when she was walking up the road and we had a winch. I'll never forget it.

I'd been sitting in the Community Centre's TV room watching the Clint Eastwood film *Heartbreak Ridge*. I swear that's true. It was freezing outside and my mates and I had nothing to do. So we hijacked the TV room, which was for the old folk in the scheme, and sat down to watch the film. It was shelter for us and kept us off the street. As I walked out after, I met Caroline and that was how we started. Who says romance is dead?

I'm proud to say that – as much as it hasn't been plain sailing – Caroline and I are still on good terms, despite living apart. We see and speak to each other most days and I spend a lot of time with my two kids. She's had to put up with a lot – let's just say, we've had our ups and downs as a couple.

We've been together now for twenty-one years and got married in 2000 at the Crutherland House Hotel in East Kilbride. It was a special day. Barry Ferguson, Craig 'Oz' Moore, Derek McInnes, Gordon 'Jukey' Durie and a few other players were all there with their wives and it was great. It was one of the best days of my life.

My ma was there too, and I'd like to think she had a good time as well, watching her boy getting hitched. Family means a lot to me, especially since I've had children of my own. I would never want my own kids to go through some of the stuff I've had to, and that has to be my aim in life now, to provide as best as I can for them, which isn't always easy. People probably think I earned enough money from my football career that I never have to work again. But they couldn't be more wrong.

2

KICKING A BALL

ALL I ever wanted to do as a kid was play football. And I knew that when I was older I wanted to do it for a living. It was all that mattered to me and I didn't care about anything else. I've been kicking a ball for, quite literally, as long as I can remember.

On a Sunday in Castlemilk, older guys – and I mean proper men – used to play on the pitch at my school, Windlaw Primary, and at just eleven I was playing with them. That's when I knew I could play. Because even at that age, the old bastards were trying to boot the shit out of me as I ran past them with the ball to score. I loved those games. It was rough at times, but I wouldn't have missed them for the world and they helped me become a better player. They made me tougher physically and also improved my skill level. My touch and close control became better – because you didn't get a minute on the ball before one of these guys was right up your backside. I had started playing for my school team when I was in Primary 3. We weren't a bad side at that time and we had a cracking player called Willie Patrick who I played alongside.

From the age of about seven, my ambition was to be a footballer. But there were a lot of good players in Castlemilk at that time, and at my school in particular. One thing that sticks in my mind about my debut for Windlaw was the strips we had. They were big, heavy *rugby* shirts. In the school colours of maroon and blue, they were horrific. For my first game it was roasting hot, and all I can remember thinking is, 'What are we wearing here?' It took us years to get rid of them, as well. It was like wearing cardboard strips. But we won that day, and I was off and running as a player.

I probably knew at the age of nine that I had a talent. I was in Primary 4 and I had scored sixty-seven goals in a season from playing as a left-winger. Willie scored more than 100, so it was no surprise that we won the league and just about every cup going that year.

I had also started playing with a wee Castlemilk team called Craig Boys' Club, who were managed by Willie's dad, Alec, and a guy called Toadie Reid.

It was at Craig BC that I started to get noticed by scouts, who came to watch our games in the hope of picking up young talent. I was beginning to get noticed and I knew it. When you're that age, you see people talking after the games and you hear your name being mentioned. I was aware that scouts were coming specifically to keep an eye on me – and I thrived on that. Several clubs showed an interest in me, but when two Castlemilk guys took over at Rangers Boys' Club Under-10s, there was only one team I was going to play for.

Toadie Reid was like a third uncle to me and was another role model, filling the gap left by my real dad. Toadie was Benny and Jim's pal and he went on to have a big influence on me. His da, 'Old Claypipe', as we knew him, used to run me to games for Windlaw. Toadie, along with Willie Patrick's da, Alec, took over at Rangers Boys' Club and that's where my association with the club really started.

There, I played with two lads, Neil Caldwell and Stuart Aitken, who both went on to become professionals. Neil made one appearance for Rangers and I'm pretty sure that on the same day Stuart was appearing for Partick Thistle. Neil also played for

Dundee United in his career, but it never really happened for him at Tannadice and he eventually chucked it.

I was only nine years old and signing for Rangers Under-10s was a big thing for me. From that moment, I played for Rangers until I left the club for Watford in 1999.

I immediately hit the ground running with Toadie and Alec in charge, and the youth coaches at Ibrox were impressed. I was playing really well and scoring a lot of goals either from midfield or up front. The coaches at Ibrox always kept tabs on the boys' club teams, in case any emerging talent came to the fore. They came to watch me a lot and liked what they saw: so much so that I signed an 'S-Form' (a 'contract' that bound me to the club until I was sixteen) when I was eleven, despite SFA rules claiming I couldn't do it until I was fourteen. That proved just how desperate Rangers were to get me snapped up and they just threw the form in a drawer at Ibrox for three years.

I was happy to commit myself to the club, and my uncles, Benny and Jim, were delighted for me. My ma and my gran took an interest in what I was doing, but they left the football side of my life to Benny and Jim. They were aware that I was doing well, but they never came to watch any of my games as a kid. It didn't bother me. Football wasn't their thing, but my uncles were immersed in it – and my progress at Rangers.

It was Benny and Jim who looked after me. Contrary to what you might think, I didn't just sign for Rangers without hesitation. Benny wanted me to keep my options open. But, looking back, I thought that getting a free pair of boots and trainers was great. I think I also got around two pounds a week in expenses, which was rubbish even then – but I wanted to sign.

That Rangers Boys' Club team was one of the best in Scotland at that age group. It was a really talented group of lads and we went from Under-10s to Under-13s undefeated until we lost to Yett Farm in the Scottish Cup at Hamilton one day.

I was excelling in the Windlaw school team at that time as well.

13

Amazingly, we won *every* game in my last season, when I was in Primary 7. That just wouldn't happen nowadays. We also won the Glasgow Cup again. I remember practically the whole school turned up on a Saturday morning for the final and we drew 3–3 against Scotstoun. I scored a hat-trick. We played them in a replay on the Wednesday night and we won 3–0. I scored another hat-trick! I felt like a hero and it did my popularity at Windlaw no harm at all.

But straight after that game I had to get to Benburb Juniors' ground in Govan, because Rangers Boys' Club had an Old Firm cup final to play against Celtic Boys' Club. Because I had played for the school earlier, I was left on the bench by Toadie and Alec. I came on as a sub at half-time with us 2–1 down to Celtic. I scored two and we drew 3–3. I felt like the hero again until it went to extra time and penalties. It was such a close contest, but it meant so much to the boys and the coaches on both sides.

So who missed the deciding spot kick in the shoot-out? Aye, me. I was heartbroken. The keeper dived to his right and saved it, but I was annoyed at myself because it was a poor penalty by my standards. In fact, it was more like a pass back to him; it was terrible. I tried to place it when I should have just put my foot through the ball and gone for power.

I had gone from being the hero of the day to wanting the ground to open and swallow me up. I'd lost us the cup and I was devastated. As a kid, that was one of the worst nights I can remember. You might think at that age a defeat wouldn't bother you, but nothing could be further from the truth. Arguably, it affects you even more than when you're a professional.

I was really down after the defeat at Benburb, as it was the first time I'd really felt a painful loss. Benny and Jim were great in picking me up, as were the coaches at Ibrox. They tried to assure me that it wasn't my fault we'd lost. It was true: if it wasn't for me, the game wouldn't even have gone to extra time, but it was difficult to appreciate that in the immediate aftermath. It was one of those moments that are so hard to take at the time but, ultimately, they help you in later life, because when you suffer a setback again, you can deal with it a lot better.

By that time I had become a Rangers fan, which hadn't always been the case when I was younger. In fact, I had spent as much time watching Celtic as I had Rangers: so much so that there has been a myth created about me that I was a proper Hoops fan growing up. It's something I always get asked by fans on both sides of the great Glasgow divide, but I can put it to bed now. The simple truth is I went to watch both Old Firm clubs play.

Uncle Benny was a Celtic man and Uncle Jim was a Rangers supporter. Despite that, Benny never once pushed me towards Celtic, even when I had the chance to go there. Jim would take me to Ibrox and Benny would take me to Parkhead – on alternate weeks, at times. I never thought of myself as supporting one team or the other. At that age, I never understood what the whole Old Firm thing meant. I was christened a Protestant, as were my uncles, so maybe it was inevitable I'd eventually lean towards Rangers. But as a kid, it didn't bother me. I loved watching football, whether it was Rangers, Celtic or any other team. And the atmosphere at Ibrox and Parkhead was brilliant, so as a young boy it was exciting for me no matter which ground I was at.

The religious side of the rivalry between both clubs is never something that I've been too bothered about. As a kid, I didn't understand it. But for as long as I remember, I've had pals and team-mates who were Catholics and, more often than not, Celtic supporters. I would never let someone's religious beliefs shape the way I feel about them or how I act towards them.

I actually had the chance to sign for Celtic when I was fourteen. Everyone in Castlemilk at that time had a 'cheque man' – a guy who came to your door with Provident cheques, which were credit that could be used in shops and paid back later – and ours was a wee guy called Davie, a great guy. He was friendly with John Jackson, whose brother Mick played for Celtic. They were very pally with Billy McNeill and were desperate to get me to Celtic Park to meet him. He was manager of Celtic at the time and I had to go on the sly.

I didn't let anyone know that I was going to Parkhead, but I went along with Benny one day, even though I'd signed the S-Form with Rangers. I was thrilled about the prospect of meeting a legend like McNeill. This guy had lifted the European Cup in 1967, so I wanted to hear what he had to say. McNeill, to this day, has an aura and a presence about him, so I was nervous but excited about seeing him.

Benny had said I should explore all of the options I had. After all, an S-Form could be cancelled without too much hassle. But when I turned up, we were told Billy couldn't make it and he'd sent his chief scout John Kelman instead. It really disappointed me and I just thought, 'Fuck it.' It was as if he couldn't make the effort to meet me, so how much did he really want me? Had he been put up to it when he didn't even know too much about me? I'm not sure, but I was gutted.

If I'm honest, I never wanted to sign for Celtic, but, at the same time, I didn't want to be ignorant. Kelman tried to persuade me to leave Rangers and go to them – but by that point my mind was made up. I wanted to be a Rangers player and I was totally committed to them. By playing for Rangers Boys' Club, I had become more of a supporter of the club. I had a real connection with Rangers, which happens when you're scoring goals and winning things with that royal-blue kit on.

As I say, I'm not denying that I went to Celtic games as a kid. I did. But I went to Ibrox as well and I don't think my affinity with Rangers can ever be questioned – certainly since I made my debut for the first team in 1993.

Around the same time I sneaked off to Celtic Park, I was beginning to make my mark at international level as well for Scotland's schoolboys. I was involved in Scotland's youth teams from the age of fourteen right through the ranks and I played in the Victory

Shield, which is always live on Sky TV and has unearthed some incredible talents through the years, like Michael Owen. It's an annual Under-15 competition involving the home nations, and I made a good start, playing against Northern Ireland in a 2–0 victory at Petershill Juniors' park.

We were due to play England next at Wembley, which would have been incredible. To play in that huge stadium, on the big, famous Wembley pitch would have been something else. But, unfortunately, I never made the trip to London with the rest of the boys, because I managed to tear my groin muscle while playing for the Castlemilk High School team. I was distraught. It was the first real injury I had suffered since I started playing football.

Because I was with Rangers Boys' Club, it was agreed that I go in to see the Ibrox physio Phil Boersma, who was brought to the club by Graeme Souness. I have to say, I didn't think Phil was a great physio. I remember him telling me to do certain exercises that convinced me I was making the groin injury even worse. I was becoming frustrated and my uncle Benny wasn't happy. Eventually, through a friend, he arranged for me to go and see Brian Scott, who was Celtic's physio at the time.

Brian stayed not far from Castlemilk, in Burnside, and he was brilliant with me. Within a couple of weeks of doing different stretches and exercises, I was on the mend and my groin was feeling much better. It didn't get me to Wembley, but I was appreciative of what Brian did for me. It was just a shame I didn't play more in that particular Scotland Under-15 side.

We had some excellent players, like Kevin Harper, who went on to play for the likes of Hibs and Stoke City, and Paul Ritchie, who played for Hearts and Rangers. Both of them, along with myself, won full caps for our country, so it was a strong side we had back then. Even then, a lot of the boys who were really talented didn't make the grade at all. At that age, though, I was so determined I'd make it as a professional.

I was doing well at Rangers and making good progress.

Obviously I was still learning the game, with the help of Benny and Jim but also through the coaching I was getting on a Tuesday and Thursday night from the coaches at Ibrox. We used to train across from the stadium at the Albion, Rangers' old training ground, which is now a giant car park. The first team would train there during the day and then the boys' club teams would be there at night. This was before the AstroTurf pitch was installed directly across from the Ibrox front door, which is still there now. The grass pitch wasn't great at the Albion, but we knew the Rangers players trained there so it was special to be learning our trade on the same park.

I remember my first-ever experience of the Albion – and it isn't a particularly pleasant memory. I had just turned eleven and we were playing an eleven-a-side game there. The Rangers youth coaches at that time were Alastair Stevenson and John Chalmers. They were two great guys and it was tragic when John took his own life in 1999, aged just forty-nine. That night Alastair and John needed someone to play right-back and, stupidly, I put my hand up and said, 'I'll do it.' I wanted to show that I could play anywhere. I was trying to impress them.

I was up against Kevin Fotheringham, who later went on to play for Rangers' reserves. He was a really good left-winger and I'd never played right-back in my life before. He tore me a new arsehole. He absolutely battered me, but it was a great learning experience for me. I thought after it, 'I'll never do that again.' I was always a central midfielder, even as a kid. I could play further forward as a striker, but I preferred midfield. I liked to create goals as much as score them, and I also loved to get stuck in.

Souness was the manager of Rangers when I was a kid, before Walter Smith eventually took over in 1991. Walter would go on to be a huge influence on me and my career, but the first time I ever met him was at Springburn Park in Glasgow. He stood at the side of the pitch with an umbrella watching the young Rangers Boys' Club team, and after it he called me over. He just had a little word in my ear as I walked off, but it was my first encounter with him. I'd seen him around Ibrox and the Albion, but I had never spoken to him.

I'll never forget it, even though he didn't say a lot. He told me if I kept working hard and doing what I was doing, I'd be fine. He said, 'We'll look after you.' That was it. But it meant a lot to me at that time, because I was only fourteen years old. He was the manager of the club, so it was a big thing for me. At the same time, I think Walter knew a lot of other clubs wanted to sign me, so it was probably a clever thing for him to do. He needn't have worried, though, as my mind was set on playing for Rangers. I had got to know everyone there and I felt comfortable.

I always felt that I would be asked to sign a professional contract with Rangers at sixteen, but I knew that if I was lucky enough to go into Ibrox full-time, it would be another huge step up for me. That's why I was so appreciative of my school, Castlemilk High, because they allowed me to leave at the earliest opportunity and start my apprenticeship with Rangers.

It won't come as a surprise to most people who know me, but I wasn't great at school. I was too mad on football; that's all my head was filled with. Even if I'd stuck in with my studies, I don't think I'd have got many qualifications, as I just wasn't interested. Basically, the school let me go four months before I was due to leave. My head teacher was a guy called Jimmy Paul, who had taken a shine to me and absolutely loved his football. He was feared by many pupils at the school, but not me – I thought he was a great man. He helped me a lot and was instrumental in getting me out early. Looking back, it was vital, because it gave me a four-month start on all the other first-year pros at Rangers.

You're always the worst player when you go full-time at a club. You think you're the best player in your age group, until you start your apprenticeship. It's like starting again. And everyone else above you at the club, from first team to reserves to first- and second-year pros – they're all ahead of you in the queue. That's a tough thing to deal with after years with your boys' club and being the best player in the team. And Rangers had so many players at that time, right throughout the club. At that point, it seemed to me like it would be really difficult to break through.

The other side to life as a young pro are the daily working duties you have to do in and around the stadium. Christ, even after I'd made it into Walter's first team he still had me doing the chores. Believe it or not, one of my first jobs on Rangers' ground staff was cleaning the gaffer's changing-room. When it came to those day-to-day duties I just couldn't be bothered with them – all I wanted to do was get out and play football. But I now know that it's all part of your grounding at a football club. Billy Kirkwood, one of the coaches, used to have to do my work for me, which he wasn't happy about. Honestly, almost every day you'd hear a big 'CHHHAAAAAARRRLLLLIIIEEEEEE' down the Ibrox corridor. It was Walter or Archie Knox bawling at me. They'd shout, 'Where the fuck are you?' Kirky would call me all the names under the sun, because he and John McGregor were in charge of the young boys. Kirky looked after me and I feel bad about it now. But he got me out of a few proper bollockings off Walter.

I can't say I ever took a real roasting from the gaffer as a young player, but I do remember playing in the 1994 BP Youth Cup final against Airdrie at Broomfield Park and we had won everything at our age level. It was the last game of the season.

We were losing 3–0 and Fotheringham scored on the stroke of half-time to make it 3–1. We came in and all of a sudden Walter was in the dressing-room.

He went absolutely fucking tonto. He raged, 'You lot want to go places at this club? Well you're going fucking nowhere, you shower of bastards.' He ordered us to get the fuck out there and sort it.

We'd only had a couple of minutes of half-time, so we were back out on the pitch waiting for the Airdrie boys to come out. He didn't even allow us to sit in the dressing-room and get a drink. Needless to say, we won 5–3; Fotheringham scored four and I got the other one. That was a relief, I'll tell you. I wouldn't have wanted to be back in that dressing-room with Walter had we lost that game.

The young boys were in awe of him at that time, as we were all trying desperately to impress him and force our way into his first-team squad. I was doing well and I could tell I was on the verge of making a breakthrough. Looking back, it was impossible for Walter not to take notice of me due to my performances for the reserves. Back then, I was a prolific goalscorer and it didn't matter whether I played up front or in midfield. I just had an eye for goal and, without sounding big-headed, I found it *easy* to score goals. That all changed when I made the progression into the first team, which was completely different. But at youth and reserve level, I was regularly on the score-sheet and I scored a lot of important goals for Rangers.

There are a couple of matches that stick out in my head, for obvious reasons. Not many Rangers players score a hat-trick in an Old Firm game against Celtic but, incredibly, I did it *twice*. On 6 November 1993, I scored an *eight-minute* treble that, as far as I'm aware, was one of the quickest ever by a Rangers player to this day. It was at Ibrox and we beat them 4–3 in a pulsating game. One of the things I remember was that Celtic had Gordon Marshall in goal that day, who was a top keeper and went on to have a really good career at Parkhead before going on to Kilmarnock.

What a day that was, and what a feeling. It was a Premier Reserve League game, but there was a big crowd at Ibrox, as there always was for any Old Firm fixture. Also, at that time, Rangers and Celtic used to drop players down into the reserves if they were coming back from injury or trying to get their fitness up. That day, we had guys like Fraser Wishart, Brian Reid and Neil Murray in the side, who all played in the first team. We also had the Russian international Oleg Kuznetsov, who was an outstanding player but who suffered a bad knee injury shortly after being signed by Souness from Dynamo Kiev.

I'll never forget the game. I scored in the 1st, 6th and 8th minutes, which is almost unheard of. I remember Robbie Fowler doing something similar for Liverpool against Arsenal at Anfield, but there aren't many players who have scored three goals in such a short space of time.

Just to win the game was brilliant, because Celtic were the opposition. To score a hat-trick within eight minutes? That will live with me forever – even if it was just for the reserves. And amazingly, I got another hat-trick against the Hoops to win the Reserve League West title at Parkhead on 15 May 1994. It was the league decider at the home of our old rivals and I remember there was a decent crowd in the ground that day as well – mostly Celtic fans this time, right enough. But we won 3–0 and we were brilliant on the day.

Big Oleg played in that one too, as did Ian Durrant, who was superb. I loved playing with Durranty. I had one of my best games in a Rangers shirt, scoring all three goals into keeper Stewart Kerr, who I knew fairly well and who went on to play in Celtic's first team under Tommy Burns not long after that.

I scored after the 27th, 44th and 70th minutes. We were just far too good for Celtic that day and it was a nice feeling – especially as a teenager – to silence the punters inside Parkhead that day.

It was another memorable match for me. Even at that age, it was special winning trophies for Rangers, and even better when it was Celtic who you were beating to get them. Those games just gave me a taste for it, and after it, I wanted more.

Goals were a big part of my game back then. I could score all sorts of goals – tap-ins, long-range shots, free kicks and penalties. I was always a threat to the opposition and I think teams knew that when they came up against me. Sometimes they'd choose someone to specifically man-mark me, but I didn't mind. I felt like I could score in every game I played in. But even so, in the back of my mind, I always wanted to create chances for others. That's where I saw myself in the future: as a creative midfielder.

I remember Brian Laudrup being criticised at times for trying to pass to a team-mate instead of shooting, but I can understand where Lauders was coming from. He got more pleasure out of making a goal for someone else than he did from scoring it himself. I was a bit like that too.

In any case, I was making an impact and felt it was only a matter of time before Walter gave me my big chance.

3

GROWING UP

YOU grow up quick in a place like Castlemilk. You have to. That scheme – which I still frequent now when visiting my family and friends – is a tough place, and in many ways, it's about survival.

You're doing well as a teenager in Castlemilk to stay away from life's pitfalls, like drink, drugs and crime. You need a strong mind and willpower to make sure you don't go down the wrong path. And I think I had that.

I'm not going to deny that I got myself into a few scrapes along the way. I saw a lot on those streets – things I wouldn't want my own kids to see or ever be involved in – but growing up there and experiencing what I did shaped me as a person for the rest of my life. Whether people like it or not, it made me the person I am today.

There were key moments – like when I was interviewed in connection with a murder investigation – which made me realise what I had as a footballer and what I could achieve if I chose the right career path. And thankfully, I did, but only just. It would have been easy for me to become so engrossed in 'life on the street' and neglect the football. There were times when I feared that might happen.

Peer pressure is a big thing in Castlemilk. Kids get dragged into stuff they really don't want to because their mates are doing it, and before they know it, they can't get out of it. That could have happened to me.

When I was thirteen years old, I had a group of pals and we all used to hang about with each other. Occasionally, we'd have a kick-about together, but it's fair to say that football wasn't our first priority when it came to the weekends, in particular.

At first, I never once thought of us as a 'gang'. But when I look back now, I realise that's exactly what we were. It pains me to say it now, but I think we intimidated other young people in the scheme. That's what gangs do, don't they? It's about strength in numbers.

We were called the 'Shop Mob'. I know it sounds ridiculous now, but that's how everyone in Castlemilk knew us. Why were we called that? Aye, you've cracked it: we spent most of our time hanging around the local shops. I told you it was ridiculous. But that's who we were: there was a wee Shop Mob and a big Shop Mob, who were almost like our superiors. Those were the guys – or the gang – we looked up to. I wouldn't say I did personally, but most of my mates probably aspired to be in the big Shop Mob.

We were all aged between thirteen and fifteen, while they were in the seventeen to nineteen bracket. To this day, I believe all of my mates were essentially 'good' boys. But I suppose I'm going to say that, aren't I?

Rab Brown – or Rab Broon as he's known – was and still is my best pal. There was Anthony 'Ants' McConville, Andy Farrow, Tony McCormack, Peter 'Ped' Collum, Rab Docherty, Joe McQuade, Paul 'Chum' McMahon, John-Paul 'J.P.' Glynn, Brendan McGettigan, Alex Goodwin and James 'Shamo' Brannan. We were all the best of mates around that time.

We were just daft boys who, at times, would try to emulate what the big Shop Mob were doing. They had the likes of Scott 'Scout' Thompson, Billy West and Tony McGregor running about – and they made sure they looked after us if there was any trouble.

I was never a fighter when I was younger and I'm still not to this day. People might find that surprising, considering I was involved in a Castlemilk gang. But anyone who has known me all my life will know that I'm not an aggressive person who looks for bother. Don't get me wrong, I'd like to think I could handle myself, but I never went out to pick fights with anyone. I've never been that way inclined.

Of course, there was peer pressure from my own mates and the big Shop Mob, but I can honestly say that I rarely found myself in a situation where I felt I *had* to fight, or show what I was made of.

There was one incident, though, I'll never forget when I was just fifteen years old. It was probably the first proper fight I was ever in and it's not something I look back on with any pride. How it came about is laughable now, but back then it was deadly serious. I had been 'serenading', if you like, a girl from school called Michelle Thompson. I fancied her and I felt as if I was making inroads with her. I was confident that I could snare her and we'd already had a wee kiss. Let's just say I was making progress.

Anyway, I was out one night and my mates had told me that a guy called Neil Gallagher had been spouting off about Michelle on a bus. He called her a cow. Right away, I was under pressure. My pals, on telling me this, expected me to hunt him down and give him a doing. Of course, I cared for Michelle, but I had no real desire to fight anyone over her. It didn't really matter to me and I didn't know this Gallagher guy. But I felt I was expected to sort him out and my mates in the Shop Mob were only too happy to organise the scrap.

Initially it was arranged for a specific night, but at the last minute a game was organised for Rangers' youths and I couldn't make it. That put me under even more pressure.

Typically, my pals had gone to clap eyes on Gallagher and they informed me, in no uncertain terms, that he was a 'big c***'. I was thinking, 'Brilliant. Not only do I not want to fight this guy, but now I know he's going to batter me.'

In any case, I couldn't back down now, so the fight was arranged for St Julie's Primary School on a Tuesday night. I know, it sounds ridiculous, but it's true.

Sure enough, I met Neil, with a few mates by my side, in the middle of the football pitch at St Julie's. My first thought? 'He's a bigger lad than they said he was!' I asked him, 'Did you call Michelle Thompson a cow?'

Quick as a flash, he replied, 'Aye.'

I was hoping he might have answered differently and we could have left it at that, but I had no choice. I felt that in a straight square go he'd win hands down. So before he could even consider his first move, I stuck the head on him.

It didn't have too much of an effect on him, so I just lost it. I nutted him again and just dived at him, throwing punches and kicks uncontrollably. I was just giving him everything I had and, thankfully, I was quicker than him. I noticed his nose had burst open – it must have been the second header – but the bastard just kept coming back at me.

It was madness. But I was beating him and eventually, as I had him down, throwing more punches, I asked him, 'Have you had enough?' I was praying he'd say 'yes', and he did. My hand was absolutely killing me and I was just desperate to get out of there. I went straight to Ants McConville's house afterwards and quickly realised that I had broken my hand in the fight. The pain was unbearable. I went to the hospital and my worst fears were confirmed – I had fractured my hand and needed a plaster cast on it, or a stookie, as most Glaswegians call it.

But it was at that point that it dawned on me: I was due to play for the Scotland schoolboys' team just three days later. I had no option but to pull out of the squad. I can't remember who we were due to play, but I had to make up an excuse because there was no way I could have played with my hand in so much pain. I told the coaches that I'd had a bad fall and that was what caused the fracture. Again, it's not something I'm proud of and, after that night, it wasn't something I wanted to do again.

I may not have been a natural fighter but I was a smoker from an early age – and it wasn't just cigarettes. Every one of my mates was smoking at that time and, although they never forced me into it, it was something I got into very easily. I'll admit now that I got into cannabis in a big way during my teenage years, even as I was beginning to make good progress in Rangers' youth and reserve sides. Call it what you like, wacky baccy, hash, whatever – I started taking it from the age of fourteen onwards. I've never really spoken about it before now, but I won't deny it. I just tried it one night and I liked it. It was enjoyable and relaxing – I'm not ashamed to say that.

At that particular time, I wasn't a big drinker, but I really liked smoking hash and I did it regularly with all the boys for the best part of three years before I realised I had to stop for the sake of my Rangers career. I was doing well at Ibrox, I had made a big impression in the youth team and was breaking into the reserves. I had even caught the eye of Walter Smith. But when I was fifteen and sixteen, I didn't care about what the hash might do to me.

The thought of actually playing in Rangers' first team was a long way off and I was more concerned about having a good time with my mates on a Friday and Saturday night. It was only when I forced my way into Walter's team at seventeen that I knew I had to chuck it. Before that, lots of folk, like my uncle Benny and others, had told me that I was in danger of going down a potentially dangerous route, but I paid no attention to it. They'd say, 'You have to get your head together and get away from this lot.' But they were my pals and I never once felt like that. There was no chance whatsoever of me not hanging about with them just because I might end up as a Rangers player.

Listen, when I look back now, I know I haven't always made the right choices in life. I'm acutely aware of that. With hindsight, it was wrong to be smoking hash at that time and it could have had serious consequences for my football career. I'm certainly not proud of it. And one day, I'm not entirely sure why, it just dawned

28

on me: 'What if I get drug tested after a game for Rangers?' You know how strict the football authorities are when it comes to drugs nowadays. My career would have been over before it had even started if I'd been tested and results came back with traces of cannabis.

I suppose, at the point when I eventually stopped, it hit me just how much I wanted to be a footballer. I didn't want to be remembered as someone who 'could have made it' but got hooked on smoking dope instead. It was a stupid thing to do and I knew it. Thankfully for me, I never really came close to being caught in the act. I don't think Walter, or anyone at Rangers, was aware of my habit. To be honest, I mostly did it indoors when I was sitting with pals having a few cans and a smoke.

There have been loads of rumours throughout my career about me taking this drug and that drug when I was younger. But it's all bull. I won't deny that, as a teenager in Castlemilk, I was offered every drug going. I could have taken anything I wanted. In my life, there have been open-goal opportunities to take cocaine, ecstasy, acid, you name it – I could have taken it if I'd wanted to. And most of my mates did at one time or another. But I can honestly say that I resisted the temptation. Acid was especially popular among my pals at that time, but it never appealed to me. I thought the hash was enough. As well as smoking joints, I was taking buckets as well.

For those of you not familiar with that technical term, let me explain. A bucket is essentially another smoking device but is constructed using two bottles, a plastic one and a glass one, one inside the other. Like joints, it is designed to get you stoned, but with a bucket you can get high quicker.

I won't lie: I loved the feeling of it, even though I know now that it was a big mistake. When I started to feature in Rangers' first team in 1994, I just stopped doing it. It was one of the best decisions I ever made.

Obviously, drinking was a big vice for the boys in the gang

as well. And when I eventually stopped smoking hash, I started to bevvy a lot more. And I won't kid you, I like a good drink now. Because I was getting a bit of money – especially after I got £30,000 for my Rangers debut, which I'll talk more about later – I was able to buy all my mates their weekend 'cargo'. They loved it and I enjoyed being able to help them out and make sure they had a good weekend. I'm sure they would have done the same for me.

I saw a lot of horrible things on the streets of Castlemilk: fights, assaults, theft, bullying, I witnessed it all. It was, and still is, a place that's renowned for being rough, and the drink and the drugs play their part. Don't get me wrong, there are thousands of great people who live there and it has certainly yielded some successful footballers over the years. My good friend Andy McLaren had a similar upbringing to me in Castlemilk and – despite having to overcome problems in his life and his career – Andy's a big success story now. He's got his own business and he helps raise money for charity. He's coaching kids in deprived areas and has done well for himself. I'm delighted for him. The likes of Leeds United legends Eddie and Frank Gray grew up in Castlemilk, as did the ex-Liverpool and Republic of Ireland international Ray Houghton. More recently, young James McCarthy – who was born and bred in Castlemilk – has emerged as one of the biggest talents in the English Premier League. After developing at Hamilton Accies, he moved to Wigan and last year he was transferred to Everton for £13 million. It's brilliant to see kids like that, who came from my area, doing well for themselves. When I see young James play well down in England, I feel proud that he's a Castlemilk boy.

Anyway, I doubt if any of these guys didn't experience things growing up that they'd rather they hadn't.

When I was very young, I remember that I was standing at a bus stop in the scheme with a pal of mine, Barney White. We were only about eleven at the time so weren't involved in a gang or anything like that. We were just kids. Across the road, two guys were arguing with two members of the big Shop Mob. They were giving as good as they got, to be fair to them, which was unusual for us to see. But one of the boys I recognised then picked up a brick and hit this guy flush over the head with it. It sent him crashing to the deck and he was in a lot of bother. As he was lying on the ground, he shouted over to me, 'C'mon, wee man, give us a hand here.' But me and Barney just looked at each other and said, 'Sorry, pal,' and we jumped on the next bus coming up the road.

For us two, to go and help the guys who were fighting against the big Shop Mob would have been suicide for us in Castlemilk. You just didn't do that, and Barney and I were well aware of what we had to do. Our lives wouldn't have been worth living if we'd run to the rescue of the guy who'd been hit. It didn't even enter our minds to do that.

There were funnier moments with the gang, though. One that sticks out involved my mate Andy Farrow. We were standing outside Woor Ping, the local Chinese takeaway, and Andy decided he was going to steal a guy's meal off him as he came out of the shop. There was no particular reason for it, other than to bully the guy and take his food off him. Maybe Andy was hungry, but I think he just thought it would be a laugh. Again, it seems stupid now, but that was his plan. So this guy walked out of the Woor Ping and Andy shouted, 'Here you, geez your Chinky.' (It might not be very PC in today's society, but that was the language we used back then.)

Unfortunately for Andy, on this occasion he had picked the wrong guy. The boy looked at him and said, 'You want it, wee man? Come and get it.'

As Andy walked over, the guy opened up the container and smashed it into his face. It was piping hot and Andy was screaming the place down. He was so embarrassed at having a curry or chow mein splattered over his coupon, he just ran across

31

the car park towards his house in Dougrie Drive. The rest of us were rolling about, pissing ourselves laughing. I think Andy's still got a wee scar on his face from the hot food. But it was so funny at the time.

I don't recall ever feeling in real danger when I hung about with the Shop Mob. We would do daft things like get taxis and then bump the driver – jumping out without paying him. Or we'd sneak on and off the buses in Castlemilk without coughing up the fare. But the worst thing that ever happened was the murder of young Andrew Halley on 5 June 1994 at around 1 a.m. It was something I inadvertently became involved in, through no fault of my own, but the ramifications of it could have cost me my Rangers career.

I was seventeen years old and on a night out with my girlfriend Caroline and few other couples. It was nothing major, just out for a meal and a couple of drinks. We were always planning to go back to Caroline's house afterwards and I remember being in the taxi on the way there. It was after midnight on a Saturday night. I'll always remember the fact that the taxi couldn't get up Castlemilk Drive – the main road in the scheme – because it was shut off by police. There had obviously been a serious incident and the taxi had to detour via Croftfoot Road. No one could get through Castlemilk's main drag that night.

We managed to get back home okay, but the following morning it emerged that there had been a major incident the night before. There had been an argument outside Castlemilk Community Centre involving Halley, who was there for a birthday party. Apparently, two of my mates, J.P. Glynn and Peter Collum, had got involved with him, and as a result a few boys from the big Shop Mob decided to take matters into their own hands.

I'm not sure of the full story after that, but I heard that Halley and one of his uncles went to his house in Glenacre Drive to get a machete, before returning to Castlemilk Drive. I think he was drunk and things got a bit out of hand. Halley had then been stabbed with his own weapon and tragically died on Castlemillk Drive that night.

The next day, I heard that J.P. and Ped had been 'taken out of Castlemilk' to keep them out of it and away from police. In that area, in a situation like that, it wasn't unheard of.

Just over a month later, I was training with Rangers at the Albion. It was during the 1994 World Cup, and the Colombian defender Andrés Escobar had been shot dead for scoring an own goal. It was a tragic incident and reported all around the world. It was big news. I remember shouting out to the boys during a stretching exercise, 'What about that guy Escobar getting shot for scoring an OG?' Almost immediately, Archie Knox, our assistant manager, said something along the lines of, 'You'll be fucking next if you don't start cooperating with the polis.'

Archie took me completely by surprise, I didn't have a clue what he was getting at. But it made sense a couple of hours later when Walter called me into his office at Ibrox. That, in itself, wasn't too unusual, but I had a feeling something was up after Archie's comments.

Walter sat me down and said that a long-time friend of his, DCI Bob House, was the leading investigator in the Halley murder and he wanted me to help him as much as I could with information on what happened. You could have knocked me down with a feather. I was stunned. Since the night it happened, I had barely given it a second thought.

I said to Walter, 'Gaffer, I can't tell him anything because I wasn't there.'

Although I had heard from various people what had happened that night, I didn't see any of it with my own eyes. It was all just hearsay from mates, and there were different versions of events.

For some reason, the police were convinced that J.P. and Ped, among others, had come back to my house on the night of the murder. But that is categorically untrue. I didn't have a clue about the incident until the next day.

But Walter was having none of it and was convinced that I knew more than I was letting on. Clearly, his pal and leading investigator also thought I was involved in some way or was holding back information.

Effectively, Walter was asking me to be a grass. He wanted me to cough to what I'd heard and nail someone I knew had been involved in the fight with Halley. I'd be putting someone – people I knew – in the frame for a murder I wasn't sure they'd even committed.

I just couldn't do that to my mates. There's an unwritten rule in places like Castlemilk – or any housing estate in Glasgow, for that matter – that you don't grass people up.

Repeatedly, I told Walter that I couldn't help him or his mate. But I knew my refusal to talk could have serious consequences, because he wasn't happy with me.

Eventually I was questioned by the police at Aikenhead Road station, along with a few of my other mates from the Shop Mob. But I told them nothing. I didn't know exactly what had happened. I hadn't done what Walter wanted me to and, at that point, I genuinely feared for my Rangers career. At the same time, I felt as if I'd done nothing wrong but was now in the middle of something that had fuck all to do with me.

Almost everyone in Castlemilk had heard by that time who was involved in the murder, but they weren't getting quizzed by the cops – I was. I thought it was unfair of House: just because he was Walter's mate, he must have asked the gaffer to lean on me and the expectancy was that I'd grass and give him a name.

In Castlemilk, you can't be known as a grass. If I'd have coughed, about an incident I hadn't seen, I would have got myself into big trouble with my own mates and the big Shop Mob as well. Trust me, my life wouldn't have been worth living if I'd done what Walter had asked me to.

Two men who I knew well, Scott 'Scout' Thomson and Billy West, were charged with the murder of Andrew Halley. They were accused of 'repeatedly striking him on the body with a knife', which cost him his life. Scout and Billy were only twenty at the time, while Halley was twenty-two.

After a trial at Glasgow Sheriff Court, Thomson and West were jailed for two years on a reduced charge of manslaughter, as a jury had ruled that the attack was in self-defence. Halley was killed with his own weapon.

The whole episode had a real effect on me. It was serious stuff and, for the first time in my life, a light switch went on inside my head. If I was going to make something of myself and have a successful football career, I couldn't be getting caught up in that kind of thing. It wasn't just a bit of naughtiness, the kind of thing me and my mates would have a laugh about on the streets. This was murder, and Halley's death definitely had an impact on me. I didn't stop hanging around with my mates, but I certainly took a step back from it all. Part of me wanted to get away from that kind of madness.

Around the same time, Caroline announced that she was expecting a baby and I was going to be a father.

It was a big shock to me and suddenly everything seemed to be happening at the same time in my life. The murder and run-in with Walter, my breakthrough into Rangers' first team, the baby, the £30,000, a new house (more on all that later) – I must admit that it was all getting on top of me a bit. It's a lot for any teenager to take in.

Even when I did get away from Castlemilk, trouble seemed to be following me around. One incident I remember vividly got me on the front page of the morning papers, for all the wrong reasons. It was after I'd moved to Burnside. I had a Honda Prelude club car, which was quite smart at the time. I was driving to the local shops at Springhall with my mate Ricky Ward. He was my best pal Rab's brother-in-law and the three of us were really close. You'll hear more about Ricky's tragic life later. But this night, he was in the passenger's seat as we set off for the shops to buy 'fags and skins'. That's cigarettes and cigarette papers to anyone not familiar with the terminology!

This was in 1995, so I was a fully-fledged Rangers first-team player at the time. I know, I shouldn't have been smoking, but I was on this occasion. We were both stone-cold sober and wouldn't have bothered anyone. But as we drove towards the shops, two drunk guys walked out in front of us. They'd been at the local pub in Cathkin and were clearly worse for wear.

I parked up and Ricky went into the chippy for the fags. While I waited, I sat reading the paper, minding my own business. Now, crucial to his story is the fact that, in the back of my car, there was a glass bottle of tomato juice. I know it sounds weird, but whenever Rab had been on the drink, he always drank a bottle of tomato juice to finish off. Strange, I know, but that's why it was there.

Suddenly, a young kid who was no older than seven years old ran over to the car and shouted, 'Charlie, your pal Ricky's fighting in the chippy.' I panicked and the first thing I thought of was to grab the bottle of tomato juice. When I ran in to help Ricky, he was scrapping with these two drunks and had already stuck the head on one of them. To finish him off, I smacked him over the head with the bottle and knocked him to the floor. Then I cracked the other guy with a punch before we both fled the chip shop. It was crazy.

We found out later that the pair of them were Rangers fans, which made it even more ridiculous. They had been having a go at Ricky, goading him and saying he thought he was a big man driving about with Charlie Miller in his flash car. But nothing could have been further from the truth.

We got back down to my house in Burnside and, would you believe it, these two idiots were outside the back garden on the football pitches behind the house having another go. I had a set of brand-new golf clubs lying at the back door and Ricky didn't hesitate. He'd grabbed a couple and was all set for round two. At first, I was about to join him. But then, in a rare moment of clarity for me, I thought to myself, 'What the fuck am I doing here?' I said to Ricky, 'I can't do this, I play for Rangers.'

That was one of the only times in my life I put a sensible head on. I hate to think to myself now what might have happened if we'd gone out and battered these two guys with golf clubs.

Instead, I phoned the police and told them there were two troublemakers at the back of my house. They arrived and the two guys were lifted. Even as they were being driven away, they were making signs out the window indicating that they'd be back to slash me.

Of course, shortly after the police car had gone and everything had calmed down, the entire Shop Mob – all my mates – turned up en masse to lend a hand. Word had obviously reached them and they fancied a fight. But they were too late. They were gutted!

Nothing really came of the incident. The owner of the chip shop was really good with us; he knew that the guys had initially provoked Ricky and that we weren't causing any trouble. But it was on the front pages of the papers. The headline was: 'Miller Thrown at Glass Door'. That was just nonsense. I don't know how the reporter got that information, because it just didn't happen. But it wasn't a nice experience and, thankfully, throughout my playing career that kind of provocation wasn't something I experienced too often.

Looking back, these were all huge moments in my life.

I'd say it was around that time that the penny finally dropped for me, in terms of realising what a chance I had to make something of my life. So many boys like myself, from an area like Castlemilk, have probably had an opportunity like I had and thrown it away because of the teenage life they led. The hash, the bevvy, the fags, the company I was keeping: as much as it was part of me, I wanted to make sure it didn't ruin everything I'd worked for up until that point.

Listen, anyone close to me will know that I would never

37

abandon my mates, and even now I still see them. But it was time to grow up a wee bit. People ask if I was close to going the other way and saying, 'Fuck the football.' Maybe I was and didn't realise it. But if you asked me now? No, never.

Contrary to what people think, I was a good trainer and I was committed to my football. Remember, I was the only player in my Rangers BC team to really go on and be successful in the game. So, as well as a bit of talent, I must have had some willpower too.

4

BREAKTHROUGH

USUALLY when a youngster makes his debut for Rangers it's remembered for a pass he makes or goal he scores. But not me.

Whenever anyone asks me about 18 September 1993, when I started against Aberdeen at Pittodrie, the next question is: 'So what did you spend the £30,000 on?' It's incredible. Everyone knows that's what I received, as a seventeen-year-old, for playing my first game under Walter Smith twenty-one years ago. After it was revealed in the press it became common knowledge, and folk still quiz me about it now.

Of course, it was a lot of money for a teenager at that time. But the truth of the matter is, I only actually pocketed around £12,000. First off, Rangers put £10,000 of it into a pension fund for me, which I will collect later in life. By the time I was taxed on the rest, I only had about £12,000 left to spend.

I can't remember how it happened, because I didn't have an agent. But the club had it written into my first professional contract at Ibrox, that I'd receive that one-off lump sum when I made my bow. But, believe it or not, I could have earned *more* if I'd decided to leave Rangers and play elsewhere. For a start, their Old Firm rivals Celtic tried to pinch me – again – when I was doing well for Rangers' reserves. They told me if I was willing to sign for them, they'd give me £40,000 when I broke into their first team. Also, someone at Spurs got in touch with my uncle Benny around the same time and said I'd pick up £80,000 if I'd quit Glasgow for London.

Also, even earlier, when I was still with Rangers Boys' Club, I recall playing in a youth tournament in Birmingham, which was organised by Aston Villa. The Villa chairman was Doug Ellis at the time, who was at the event watching his own club's talented kids. But I had played really well and must have caught Ellis's eye. I've been told that he got hold of Alec Patrick and informed him that he'd be willing to pay Rangers £250,000 for me. Obviously, I'd have been looked after as well. That would have been an unbelievable amount of money for an untried kid. But Alec tells the story that – being a die-hard Bluenose – he was so scared of Rangers losing me, he didn't even tell anyone at Ibrox about Ellis's bid!

Looking back, I feel proud that such huge clubs were willing to fork out that kind of money for me at such a young age. I must have been doing something right. But, at the time, it just washed over me. I was only concentrating on Rangers and I was desperate to impress Walter.

Unfortunately, that day at Pittodrie wasn't one of them. I didn't expect to make my Rangers debut at seventeen. In fact, it came as a complete shock to me. But not many people know that I should have played for the first team a few days *before* that game against Aberdeen.

Rangers were playing Levski Sofia in a Champions League qualifying tie in September '93. Walter told me I had a chance of being involved in the first leg at Ibrox and I was stunned. He told me that I had to be ready and gave me the details of the training schedule for that week. The day before the game against the Bulgarians, we were due to train before getting a bus from Ibrox to a city-centre hotel. My uncle Jim was supposed to be picking me up, but he was forty minutes late for me.

When I finally got over to Ibrox, the bus was leaving. They had waited long enough for me and Walter went absolutely mental. He had a real go at me and I was totally gutted, as were the reserve coaches, John McGregor and Billy Kirkwood. I really felt that I'd let them down because they had been trying to promote me and push me towards the first team for a while. I got on great with them and they were really disappointed.

My uncle Jim claims he got the times mixed up and he was devastated as well. I didn't want to blame him, but I was close to tears. Needless to say, I played no part in the Levski tie and I wondered how long it would take me to fight my way back into Walter's thoughts.

He probably thought 'fuck him' after I'd turned up late. And he'd have been right. But I think he wanted to see a reaction from me – to see just how much I wanted it.

So, with the team decimated by injuries, I was named in the squad for Aberdeen on the Saturday, three days later. I'll always remember we stayed in the Skean Dhu Hotel and I genuinely didn't think anything of it. I was convinced I was there just to carry the hampers or had been taken as an extra squad man. I thought Walter was maybe including me just to give me a wee taste of what it was like to be around the first-team boys.

I remember sitting in the away dressing-room at Pittodrie as he read the team out and my name was in it. I couldn't believe it – I was going to start up front with big Mark Hateley. I'm not sure if I was scared, but I know I was really nervous and it showed in my performance that night.

If I'm honest, I didn't do myself justice in any of my first few games for Rangers – I featured two more times that season. I showed too much respect, not just to the people I was playing against but also to the guys I was playing with for Rangers.

That night at Pittodrie, I was up against Alex McLeish of Aberdeen. He was an experienced, commanding centre-half who had won everything with the Dons and had earned loads of Scotland caps. I didn't even regard myself as a striker back then, so it was a daunting task. The Rangers team was: Ally Maxwell in goal; a back four of Gary Stevens, Dave McPherson, Steven Pressley and Davie Robertson; a midfield of Trevor Steven, Stuart McCall, Ian Ferguson and Pieter Huistra; with myself and Mark up top.

But I was completely out of my depth that night, I admit that, and we lost 2–0. I'm sure our keeper Ally Maxwell dropped one that Duncan Shearer scored, then big Elvis, Steven Pressley, scored an own goal.

I think my first touch for Rangers landed ten yards away from me, and the pitch was poor, which didn't help. Pittodrie is one of the toughest grounds to go to as a Rangers player, so it was a baptism of fire for me.

Aberdeen were a decent side then as well. We were struggling with injuries – that's why I was involved – so it wasn't the ideal time to make my debut for the club. But I was only seventeen years old, I had just started my second year as a pro, and I felt there would be more chances for me. After that, I knew I had to take them.

Big Mark tried to help me that night at Aberdeen. He was a legend for Rangers and, as time went on, we developed a good understanding on the pitch. We would link up well for Rangers in the future, but not on that occasion.

It was no surprise that I was left out of the side for our next game, against Hibs at Ibrox, which we won 2–1. In fact, I didn't feature again until three months later when I came on as a sub against Raith Rovers at Stark's Park.

I knew, within myself, that I was edging closer to the first team. By that stage, I felt I had outgrown the reserve side and I believed I was ready. The question was, did the manager?

After drawing with Raith 2–2, I didn't play again until the second-last game of the campaign, away to Kilmarnock when we'd already clinched Rangers' sixth title on the trot by that point. Rugby Park was always a notoriously hard place for Rangers to go at that time and Killie had to win that day to seal their top-flight survival.

Their league position was surprising because, against Rangers, they were always busy as fuck and a nightmare to play against. The likes of Ally Mitchell and Mark Reilly used to run around like mad when we were in town.

Their left-back, Tom Black, scored a free kick to beat us 1–0 that day, but I had played better than I did at Pittodrie. At seventeen, I had started two games and come off the bench in one – but we hadn't picked up a victory in any of them!

After that Kilmarnock game, though, I made a conscious decision ahead of the following season, which I knew would be a big one for me. I just said to myself, 'Fuck it – if I get another chance, I'm not going to hold back.' I don't mean that I was planning to disrespect my team-mates or my opponents, but I decided there and then that whenever I put on a Rangers shirt again, I was going to go out and play my own game – and not worry about who I was playing with or who I was up against.

As for the £12,000, you're probably wondering what I did with it. Well, apart from sending my gran away to Australia on holiday to see relatives – which cost around £4,000 – I pretty much blew it. I know that won't surprise most people. But I did what you'd expect a seventeen-year-old to do with that kind of money.

I spent £4,000 on my first car as soon as I passed my driving test. It was an Audi 80 – and it was written off after just a *week*! I was on my way to training one morning and a guy ran into the back of me at the traffic lights on Mosspark Boulevard, near Ibrox. He got out and, as we were exchanging insurance details, I could smell alcohol on his breath. He was stinking of booze. My team-mate at Rangers, Pieter Huistra, just happened to be driving past and noticed I'd been in an accident. Pieter got out and he knew the guy had been drinking right away. He urged me to wait for the police to arrive so they could arrest the driver, but I didn't want that.

Again, it was probably the wrong thing to do but I didn't want to get the guy into trouble. So I just got his details and let him drive off. It was stupid because I realise now that he could have caused another accident and seriously injured someone. But it's just not in my nature to get people into trouble or get the police involved. That's probably down to my Castlemilk upbringing. My motor was fucked, but thankfully I got the £4,000 back and the club gave me a company Honda after that.

I spent most of the money on myself and my mates. I don't regret that, because I was a daft wee boy walking around a housing scheme with about £9,000 in my bank. It was a great feeling to be able to go to a cash machine and lift out the maximum it would allow and not have to worry about it. That was good. But I didn't show off; I've never been that type of person. I had a good laugh with it, although it was also around that time I started gambling more.

I loved a bet when I was younger. I still do. But I've never quite understood how I got so into it, because at first I hated horse racing. My uncle Jim loved it and still does now. Jim would stay at my gran's house a lot and I'd be watching the cartoons after school when he would charge in with a carrier bag. In it, he'd have about ten bags of crisps, five bars of chocolate and two bottles of Irn-Bru. He'd turn the TV over to the horse racing – and wouldn't give me a single bit of his goodie bag!

I was only about eight years old at that time. And from then, I didn't like horse racing. At that time I didn't realise you could win money from it. In fact, I know now you definitely *can't* win money from it. But I had my first bet at fifteen, just a football coupon. I'd hang around the shops with my mates and, as one of the older-looking ones, I'd get in to the bookies to put a line on. That was probably the worst thing that ever happened to me.

I remember my first-ever winner. I'll never forget the name of the horse, 'Catherine's Well', and I had a fiver on it at 14/1. I don't even think I meant to pick that particular one, but what a feeling when it won. I thought, 'This is easy money.' But I think people always win their first-ever bet, don't they?

The bookies are lucky bastards when it comes to that. That's when I first got the gambling bug. But it shouldn't have been allowed to happen, I shouldn't have had the time to bet, because that year, between the ages of seventeen and eighteen, was one of the most monumental of my life. On the playing side, I had just made my Rangers debut and was planning on being a regular in Walter's team the following season. And off the pitch, I had so much going on. My girlfriend Caroline was pregnant, I was about to buy my first house and I had no idea that I'd lose my gran to illness.

I knew I had to wise up a bit, but I found it difficult to drag myself away from the carefree life I had led until that point. Instead of doing the right thing, I'd still be spending all my spare time with my mates, especially after I got that £12,000 and I had played in Rangers' first team. I'd lose £200 in an afternoon at the bookies and not think anything of it. I know now that was wrong and unfair on Caroline. It might not sound like a lot of money now, but twenty-one years ago, for a seventeen-year-old who had never had anything, believe me, it was a lot of cash to throw away.

I remember being in my gran's house the day Caroline told me I was going to be a father. It was before I'd even made my Rangers debut. She walked in and said she had something to tell me: she was pregnant. We were so young. Incredibly, she said to me that if I didn't want anything to do with the baby, she would understand, but she was keeping it no matter what.

It was a big shock to me, but I would have never walked away from it. Caroline was only eighteen and there was never any doubt that I'd stand by her. But at that stage of my life I still thought my dick's main purpose was pissing against walls. Listen, I never expected to be a father at eighteen years old. And I'm ashamed now when I think that while Caroline was living with our daughter, Demi, I was staying with my mate Rab Brown. I know now that I should have been with them.

It sounds like a terrible thing to say, but there were times when I didn't actually recognise the fact that I had a kid. I was too busy just living my life – playing football and having a carry-on. The magnitude of having a baby didn't really hit me. I think it hits you more when you're thirty-five than it does when you're eighteen.

I remember telling my uncle Benny first, and his first question to Caroline was: 'Is it his?' He didn't mean it in a bad way, but she ended up having a fall-out with him over that comment. I can understand why, because no lassie likes to hear that. But I can also understand now that Benny was just trying to protect me. As soon as he knew it was definitely mine, he loved Demi just as much as everyone else in the family did. He'd have wanted me and Caroline to wait until we were twenty-five or thirty before we had kids, but the reality was we were going to be teenage parents and we had to deal with that.

Benny always said the right things and I just didn't listen to him. I regret that now. I remember he'd always say, 'You can live your life after football.' And he's 100 per cent right, but I paid no attention to it at all during my time at Rangers. He told me that for a long time, but I didn't heed his warnings.

Caroline had got a house in Dunagoil Avenue in Castlemilk. We were boyfriend and girlfriend, but, to be honest, I think she's probably glad I didn't move in with her right away, because she needed a bit of space herself.

She's a brilliant mum and a good woman; there's never been any question about that. She had a fairly smooth pregnancy with Demi and I remember going to scans at the hospital and things like that. But I regret not being there for her more at that time. I was around far more when we had our second child, Jordan, four years later, because I was a lot more grown up by then.

I'll never forget Demi's birth, though. At that point they had

TVs in the delivery rooms at Rutherglen Maternity Hospital and I remember that I was glued to *Question of Sport*.

It was Friday, 13 May 1994. My uncle Benny brought me up barbecue spare ribs from the local Chinese restaurant and I was making Caroline jealous, eating them in front of her while she was lying in bed trying to have the baby. 'You bastard,' she was screaming! But I was telling her, she had to hold on until 14 May because that was my gran's birthday. Sure enough, it was 12.45 on the Saturday morning when she had the baby and I was delighted Demi had the same birthday as my gran.

Typically, before she was born, I had given my mates £20 to get me a carry-out for the celebrations afterwards. It was quarter to one in the morning, but I think I was out of the hospital within half an hour and back up in Castlemilk.

There was nothing more I could do. Demi had a bit of jaundice, so they were taking her away to a different part of the hospital, and Caroline was knackered. I was probably being a bit selfish, but my mates had bought me two Black Pils and a bottle of MD 20/20. I never drank anything like that and I was slaughtering them for it. My carry-out at that time was always six cans of Budweiser and a quarter bottle of vodka. I'd drink three Buds, three vodkas and I'd be sleeping. I couldn't drink – and the boys would finish the rest of it for me.

So that was how I celebrated Demi's birth. It's probably not what you'd expect from a footballer who'd just broken into Rangers' first team. But that was me.

Away from 'family' time, I was the same.

I was still, in essence, a Youth Training Scheme (YTS) boy at Ibrox, even though I'd broken into the first team. The days were fairly long and I wouldn't get home till late in the afternoon. But myself, Neil Caldwell and Stuart Ayton – if we didn't have a reserve game the next day – would get the subway into St Enoch Square in Glasgow and have a few pints in the Times Square pub. We were only seventeen and it was the wrong thing to do, and as stupid as it sounds, I used to *hate* the pints of lager in there: they were horrible. But I was just doing it because I thought I could handle it and it was the cool thing to do. I'd have three or four lagers and I'd feel blazing drunk. I didn't appreciate that, as I was making a name for myself, I shouldn't be doing stuff like that.

My life was changing, but it was as if I didn't know it.

When I eventually signed a pro contract and was training every day with Walter and the first team, I'd have a lot more time on my hands after training to drink and gamble. But by then everyone in Glasgow knew who I was.

I was oblivious to it at the start. People were recognising me, but I didn't realise it. That might sound strange to people but I've never been a big-headed guy. I never once strutted about thinking, 'I play for Rangers' – that just wasn't me. So it was difficult to understand why people knew who I was. I'd keep doing and saying what I wanted, even in public, not thinking for a minute that strangers might notice or take offence.

When I was first stopped for an autograph in the street, I was embarrassed. People in the bookies would ask for a photo with me, but I didn't appreciate the significance of that change in my profile. I still thought I could just smoke a fag whenever I wanted to – that was something I'd done since I was fifteen – and no one would bat an eyelid. Much later in my career, myself and big Jörg Albertz would sit in the Ibrox dressing-room toilet before a game and have a quick puff.

When I started playing in the first team, I knew I had to give up the hash, which I had also smoked since I was young. I just wish I hadn't started smoking the odd cigarette as a replacement. I just thought that I was young, fit and I was training every day, so it wouldn't be a problem. It would only be a couple a day, but Walter suspected I was smoking from very early on. Thankfully, in the early days, I never got caught out too badly.

I did a few stupid things, I'm sure, but nothing that got me into serious trouble, although there was one incident that could have had serious ramifications for me and my future at Rangers.

Demi was born the day before the final day of the 1993/94 season, but I wasn't involved in the squad, who were preparing for the 1994 Scottish Cup final against Dundee United the following week. The club were going for a double treble, with the league already clinched, and that hadn't been done before in the club's history. The closest they had ever come to achieving that feat was in the '70s when, with Jock Wallace in charge, they won two trebles in the space of three seasons.

I wasn't involved at Hampden and we lost 1–0 to a Craig Brewster goal that won it for the Arabs. Instead of being at Hampden, just a couple of days after Demi's birth I was off to Groningen, in Holland, for an end-of-season tournament, or should I say 'jolly', with the reserve team. We had won a treble of our own that year: the league, the BP Youth Cup and the Glasgow Cup. The team at that time included myself and the likes of Greg Shields, Scott Wilson, Derek Rae, Stuart and Neil.

But that trip to Holland reminds me of one of the biggest regrets of my career. The coaches, Kirkwood and McGregor, had told us that, as a reward for our success that season, we could go there and 'let our hair down' a bit. We weren't about to defy them on that score and we got up to all sorts. About 80 per cent of the squad were all smoking dope in Groningen. The ones who weren't were smuggling booze back to their rooms.

We were there to go and drink. To have a laugh and a good time, those were our instructions. It was a 'team-bonding session'. For the first three nights, we were out bevvying, but somehow managed to win every game in the tournament. All of a sudden, Kirky and McGregor told us, 'Listen lads, we might actually have a chance of winning this.' So we stayed off the drink for two nights – and got battered by Ajax 3–0, who had the likes of Clarence Seedorf and Patrick Kluivert in their team.

We had done really well, but after that defeat it was back to enjoying ourselves again. Kirky always told us he didn't care if we were drinking away from the hotel, as long as we didn't bring any of it back with us.

But one of the boys was caught with a litre bottle of vodka in his room. That didn't please Kirky. He was raging, and it prompted him to start searching everyone's rooms.

A few of the boys had been in my room, which I shared with Stuart, smoking a joint earlier in the day. We went out and left half a joint in an ashtray under one of the beds. Later on, I came back so drunk that I didn't even touch it. I just went straight to my bed and was out for the count right away. But Stuart came in after me and decided to smoke the fucking thing. Kirky had been waiting up for boys to come in and he caught him with it, red-handed. He decided then that it was Stuart's joint and that he was solely responsible for it. But it wasn't – almost everyone had been having a puff just hours before.

In the morning, I wanted us to hold our hands up and say, 'We were all doing it.' We could have taken collective responsibility and all taken the rap for it. But Stuart was saying, 'No, I'll take the blame, it'll be fine.' But it wasn't. Stuart had been promised another year's contract at Rangers after the cracking season we'd had, but after Kirky found him with that joint, he took the decision that the contract was being taken away from him.

No one owned up to it, but I wish we had. I was absolutely gutted for Stuart and it was the end for him at Rangers. I still feel bad about that to this day.

Eventually, when you're playing every week in big games, it dawns on you that you have to behave in a certain way as a Rangers player, but at that stage I was still just on the fringes so it hadn't really hit home yet. I wasn't aware that if I'd been caught drinking or smoking, it might get back and I'd be in big bother.

People ask if 'Old Firm fame' changed me. But I can categorically say that it didn't. For a start, I would never read the papers or look for articles about myself. After my debut at Aberdeen,

I didn't even go out and buy a paper – mainly because I knew I'd had an absolute stinker of a game! But also because, at that time, I didn't believe any sports writer would know more about football than me. If someone outside of Ibrox had said that I was shite, it wouldn't have bothered me in the slightest because my attitude would have been, 'What do you know?' I now accept that the game is all about opinions and not everyone will agree with mine. That's football – and people can have completely different views on the same game.

My family were proud when I made the breakthrough at Rangers, especially my uncles, Benny and Jim, who'd had such a massive influence on my career. They weren't surprised that I'd 'made it'. My ma wasn't into football, but she knew that what I'd achieved at such a young age was a big thing.

It was becoming clearer to me as well that to progress at Rangers and do well, I had to try to take myself away from Castlemilk. I loved my pals and I could never just blank them. But, after Demi was born, it was important that, along with Caroline, we moved out of the scheme and into a house.

We managed to get all of two and a half miles away, to Burnside!

Seriously, moving into my first house was a big deal for me. I was trying to distance myself from Castlemilk and my mates to concentrate more on my career. But it was still too close. It sounds ridiculous now, but I convinced myself this was the 'big move away'.

When my gran had gone to Australia to visit her family for a few months previously, I should have gone to stay with Benny in Bishopbriggs. It would have got me right out of Castlemilk and he'd have kept me right. But I didn't. What did I do? My first thought was to go and stay with my pal Rab for the best part of a year. I loved it.

His family were great with me. Wee Jimmy Brown was Rangers-mad and loved football and his wife Rena didn't give a toss about it. I'd known them since I was six years old. I could

51

have stayed at my ma's around the corner from my gran's, but I chose to have a better laugh at Rab's house.

I don't know why I did that. I was well looked after, but I should have gone to Benny's – I know that now. Looking back, I think I might have been a bit scared to leave Castlemilk.

Anyway, after Caroline had lived for a few months on her own with Demi, I got my head together and Burnside was our destination. I'd bought a two-bedroom house for around £52,000 and Benny had helped me with the mortgage and stuff like that, as I didn't have a clue.

Demi was still a baby when we moved there. To be honest, my mates knew, even more than me, that I had to go. I was just trying to be too loyal to them. One of their best pals was 'moving away'. They didn't want me to, but they knew it was best for me.

I was trying, I really was, to screw the nut and focus on my career. But it quickly became apparent that the distance between Castlemilk and Burnside was never going to keep me away from my pals.

Every week at the new house, we'd have a 'Super Sunday' and they'd all come down. I tell you, my neighbours must have hated those Sunday afternoons. Beer, kebabs, pizzas: you name it, we had the lot. I should say that I'm embarrassed by that, but I can't, because I'd be lying if I didn't say those days were brilliant.

I had tried to make sure by moving there that I wasn't with my mates every day, but I decided Sunday was going to be my day, our day. Watching football, having a drink and generally enjoying a good time. On a Saturday night, Caroline and I would maybe have a wee couple's night. But I'm a man's man, and Sunday was what I really looked forward to.

Caroline always went out on a Super Sunday. She knew it was my day, a guy's day. When she'd come in later on, we'd all be lying pissed and she had a job on trying to get them in taxis home. I'd be as bad as anyone. I knew I had training the next morning, but that never really bothered me. I was young and fit at the time.

Simon Donnelly actually stayed in Burnside at the same time as me. He was Celtic's version of Charlie Miller, a young local boy who had broken into the Celtic first team at an early age and was regarded as a top prospect. We had two grass football pitches behind our houses and Simon used to be out there on a Sunday afternoon. He'd be stone-cold sober, honing his skills, practising his technique. Then all of a sudden, we'd all burst out of my house and go for a kickabout, absolutely steaming drunk. All my mates would have my old Rangers and Scotland tops on, trying to have a sly kick at wee Simon.

It was all quite good-natured and Simon's a good lad. He's a quiet lad but a good guy, and he took it in good spirit. God knows what he must have really thought at the time, though.

Most of his mates were Rangers fans and loads of mine were Celtic supporters. It was crazy. We couldn't get near them because we were half-jaked. But that was a Super Sunday; that was what it was all about, right?

Apart from my uncle Benny, no one ever said to me, 'Charlie, you need to get a grip, you're going to throw your career away.' I suppose, no one except my mates really knew what I was getting up to away from Rangers.

That was just my life at the time. Sometimes a Super Sunday rolled into a 'Mad Monday'.

Football has changed so much now. I still reckon, even your top players now will have a drink, but the difference is, they'll do it at the right times. They'll still have a night-out – everyone does. But I'd do it at all the wrong times.

I'm always asked if any of the senior players at Rangers ever got hold of me in those early years and gave me a stern talking-to, a pep talk to keep me on the straight and narrow. But they didn't. I'm not saying I wanted them to or whether they were right or wrong. It was my career, my life. But at no point did one of the experienced boys have a quiet word with me.

Listen, I respect Richard Gough as a person and he was an

immense player for Rangers, a brilliant captain. But Goughie was all about Goughie at that time. With Coisty – who I still love to this day – you had to make an appointment to speak to him, he was so busy. He's still like that now!

Big Mark was another huge figure in the dressing-room but I never really knew him as a person, just as a team-mate. Myself and Mark came from different backgrounds and, at times, I felt he spoke down to me a bit. He maybe felt I was a bit beneath him, me being the new kid and him an experienced pro.

I think Brian Laudrup said in a newspaper article not so long ago that he tried to talk some sense into me, but I don't remember Lauders ever saying anything to me about how to be more professional off the pitch.

Andy Goram ('the Goalie', as we called him) and Durranty were just like me in many ways, so they weren't going to give me lectures on how to live my life. And Ian Ferguson probably wanted me to carry on, because I was keeping him out of the team!

Walter? He thought I needed a kick up the arse, as opposed to an arm around my shoulder or a cuddle. I know some people might think that sounds ridiculous and that it has to come from within. I think Walter could have helped if he'd taken a different approach with me. If he'd got hold of me and said, 'Listen, son, you've got a chance here, don't blow it,' then I might have listened. But I always seemed to get a rollicking, or a threat, from the gaffer. Or he'd just drop me from the team altogether.

I loved those Super Sundays with my pals. I was still a kid and I didn't realise that, as a footballer, it was the wrong thing to be doing. There was never a point I thought, 'I have a great chance here as a professional to carve out a fantastic career at Rangers.' I just didn't think: that was my biggest problem.

To this day, I'm probably still trying to justify those times, but I accept I didn't lead my life properly at that stage of my career. My uncle Benny tried to tell me all the time. But he knew he could only go so far with me – he reached a point and then realised that no matter what else he said, it would make no difference. Even with a baby in tow, I didn't have a care in the world. I wasn't worried about anything, but, little did I know, tragedy was around the corner.

I've spoken about how close I was to my gran and how I spent my entire childhood living with her. So when she died in February 1998, I was devastated.

I was still eighteen and she'd came back from that long holiday in Australia, which I'd paid for with my debut money. She seemed fine when she got home and she'd loved her time over there. But it seemed to me that only a very short time later she had died. To this day, I still find it strange and hard to understand.

As far as I can remember, she wasn't ill. But she went to the doctors for a run-of-the-mill check-up and they told her she had cancer. It all happened so quickly. To this day, it's still a blur. It was horrible and I don't know if I've ever really got over it. This is the first time I've ever spoken about her death, and even now I'm not comfortable with it, because she meant so much to me. I find it hard to open up about it. I suppose the only saving grace is that neither my gran nor I suffered from her having a long, drawn-out illness. I didn't even know that she wasn't well.

I miss my gran so much, even now. Her death is still hard to comprehend all these years on. It was the first time in my life I'd dealt with loss. A real loss.

Around the same time, a young cousin of mine, Rebecca Miler, also sadly passed away. That hit me hard too, as she was my uncle Jim's daughter, and we were quite close.

Rebecca had cystic fibrosis. She was a lovely wee lassie. She seemed to be at Yorkhill constantly for treatment and she was only a child when she passed away. I've always felt that because I watched Rebecca being buried, her casket going into the ground, it was somehow worse than when my gran was cremated. Or maybe it was just because I was so numb after my gran's death.

I can still visualise my gran's funeral at Linn Crematorium. It's an experience I never want to go through again. The curtain closed and my gran was gone.

5

WALTER AND ME

LET me make one thing clear: I love Walter Smith, both as a man and as a manager. He was the gaffer who gave me my big chance at Rangers. To throw me into a multimillion pound team at the age of seventeen shows that he had faith in me. Without Walter, I wouldn't have won nine-in-a-row at Rangers. Who knows? I might not even have made it as a footballer.

But, despite all that, I have to be honest. And, to this day, I still feel a bit of resentment towards one of Scottish football's legendary managers. I feel he could have handled me better as a kid at Ibrox. I think he could have guided me more. People will say that guiding myself was my responsibility, and maybe they're right. But, in my opinion, Walter could have been more of a father figure to me during my time at Rangers.

He did certain things that still rankle with me, even now. Yet our relationship got off to a good start. I'll never forget our first encounter when I was only fourteen or fifteen and I was playing a youth team game in Springburn, Glasgow. When I was a kid at Rangers, the head of youth was a guy called Gordon Neill, who I got on well with. When he left the club, I remember being worried about who they'd bring in to replace him. But that night in Springburn, I came off the pitch and Walter was there. I was stunned when he pulled me aside.

Walter assured me my future was at Rangers, no matter who was going to replace Alastair. At that point, he hadn't been in the job that long after taking over from Graeme Souness, so for him to single me out meant a lot. It was reassuring for me, because I was concerned that a new coach might not fancy me as a player.

So, Walter and I got off to a great start together – but it wasn't quite as smooth as that for the rest of my time at Ibrox.

Walter is quite rightly regarded as one of our game's top bosses. His achievements at Rangers are unparalleled in two separate spells at the club. He also proved to be a huge success as Scotland's national coach and was rated by doyens of the game like Jock Stein and Sir Alex Ferguson. But I rarely got to see Walter's qualities on the training pitch because at Ibrox he didn't take sessions very often. He left it to Archie Knox and Rangers first-team coach Davie Dodds, but I'm still not sure why. You see it with a lot of older managers, don't you? They take a step back and manage rather than actually coach.

That wouldn't be me. If I'm ever a manager, I'd prefer to be more hands on. If I was sacked, I'd want to be sacked for what *I* did – not one of my staff. Anyway, it was always Archie and Davie who took training at Rangers.

Like Walter, I loved Archie as a guy, but, I have to say, I thought his training was awful at times. Some days, I'm convinced, Archie just made things up on the spot. I'll never forget the day he had us trying to 'beat' men – without a ball. I know that sounds ridiculous, but I swear it's true. It was the craziest things I've ever been involved in. There were eleven of us on the pitch with no ball and no opposition. We had to run around acting out a game, while Archie shouted 'take him on' or 'switch it'. I remember looking over at Derek McInnes and I could tell we were both thinking, 'What the fuck is this?'

I just found some of Archie's routines ridiculous, and when they didn't go well, he would go mental and tell us we'd be back out in the afternoon. But the likes of Gazza and Laudrup had their suits on within ten minutes of finishing. Walter would over-rule Archie and tell us we could go home.

I remember being in the squad for a Champions League group game against the Swiss side Grasshoppers Zurich in the 1995/96 campaign. I didn't play, but we got hammered 3–0 over there. It was a terrible result and performance, which got us a lot of criticism from the fans and media. We didn't get back until the following day and the players who had been involved were allowed to go straight home to their families.

But, despite having a kid myself, me and the rest of the boys who hadn't played were ordered to train with Archie and John 'Bomber' Brown. We were pinging balls about in another stupid exercise and I asked Bomber, 'Why are we getting punished when we didn't even play last night?' I was annoyed about it. Then, sure enough, the next day Walter said to me, 'You, come here – are you trying to fucking undermine me?' He ordered me to report with the reserves the next day. I was at Tannadice with the stiffs while the first team beat Hearts 4–0 at Ibrox!

I can't be too critical of Archie because he's a great man and he was brilliant for that Rangers dressing-room: he was great at fostering team spirit and had a terrific sense of humour. People have asked me if he was the link between the players and Walter, but Archie was more than that: he had a big say in training and tactics.

Davie was more of a 'go-between' for the players. He's a top bloke and I still feel that he was harshly dealt with by the club. In 1997, he was bumped off the coaching staff in favour of the Dane Tommy Moller Nielsen, who came in from Boldklubben. Davie fell out of the game after that, which was a real shame because he played a big part in our success at Rangers.

All Tommy did was the warm-up before training and games. Davie used to take a few of the boys out in the afternoons to do crossing and finishing exercises. In his day, Doddsy was a top striker for Dundee United and Aberdeen. Granted, he was also the ugliest guy I've ever met! Doddsie wasn't nicknamed 'the Elephant Man' for nothing. But, seriously, you could learn off him. I always remember him telling me that if a cross comes in from the right, hit it with your right foot, and vice versa if it was on the left. It sounds like a simple thing, but he hated when strikers allowed the ball to run across their body onto their stronger foot, because it meant the defender could get in and put a block in. It was a clever piece of advice and something I always kept with me wherever I played.

Ultimately, though, Walter was the main man and it was him I had to impress to earn my first professional contract at eighteen years old. That was my first proper deal as a Rangers player and I was delighted that the club were putting their faith in me. At that time, I was desperate to commit myself to Rangers for as long as possible.

My Uncle Benny told me I'd need an agent to negotiate the deal. Almost every other player in the dressing-room had one, so why shouldn't I? Benny thought it was for the best. But Walter never really mentioned the need for an agent. He just wanted to get the deal done as quickly as possible and, to be fair, so did I. I was a young kid from Castlemilk and this was a major opportunity for me. I just wanted the chance to pull on that Rangers jersey on a regular basis and prove that I was good enough to play for the club.

When it came to the contract, I was convinced the club would look after me properly and give me what they thought I merited. After speaking to Walter, I decided against getting an agent – even though Benny disagreed. I'd put my faith in Walter and believed that he would sort everything out. Even if he wasn't deciding on the exact details of the deal, I was sure the club would see me right. I don't think Walter was a big fan of agents for young kids, particularly as it tended only to be the established first-team players who had agents back then.

Obviously, Walter was a Rangers man through and through

and the good of the club came first with him. With the resources he had in the squad, he probably felt that any young player had to prove himself first before he could think about commanding top-line wages.

However, looking back, if I'd had an agent I think I'd have been able to get a much better deal. People might think I was on loads of money at Rangers, right through the charge to nine-in-a-row. But I wasn't. In 1994, I signed a 'bumper' five-year contract at Ibrox – a dream come true for me. However, the deal structured for me wasn't exactly 'bumper'. Most people will find this hard to believe but my new five-year contract would see me earn £600 per week in my first year, £700 in my second, £800 in my third, £900 in my fourth and £1,000 in my fifth.

Now, I'm not trying to decry that type of salary – it's good money for a teenager from Castlemilk – but I had broken into the Rangers first team and I was soon keeping out international players who were on thousands of pounds more. The likes of Trevor Steven and Alexei Mikhailichenko were struggling to get a game ahead of me at that time.

To give you an example, I played twenty-three games in Rangers' seven-in-a-row season and I was only on £700 a week. I think a lot of Rangers fans will be surprised about that. Even though I was only eighteen, I had a girlfriend and baby girl to look after. I'd had to move into a new house at a young age so I had a mortgage, a car and bills to pay.

On that occasion, I just can't see how the club 'looked after me' like I had expected them to. Getting me to sign that deal was not, as I see it now, in my best interests and, looking back, I'm disappointed about what happened.

Don't get me wrong, I'm not looking for sympathy. The win bonus at Rangers around that time was £1,200 – and we were winning most games. So, on a good week in my first year, I might be earning £1,800 a week. But the weeks where I wasn't involved in the first team over the next few years were really tough for me, particularly when I began to realise what I'd signed and the money some of the rest of the boys were on.

I was still getting taxed at 40 per cent on my £600 or £700 a week, so I wasn't making a fortune. It was rubbish, in fact. There should have been money left over from the good weeks to tide me over through the lean ones, but it never seemed to work out that way, mainly because I just wasn't mature or responsible enough to make that happen at that time. So the lean weeks could be very lean indeed after tax.

If I'd had a good agent at that time then I think the financial package would have been a whole lot better. It left me feeling let down. And although I got my chance at the big time, there's no way I can see anything like that happening these days, even with young players, if they're top-class talent.

I can't help how I feel about it now and I think it was wrong. I wish I had listened to Benny. How many times have I said that already? I never listened to him and always thought he was wrong in what he was saying. But, more often than not, he was right. I believed others over him, but I was a naive young boy and I regret that now.

To be fair to the club, I had only recently signed a pro youth deal on £350 per week, so they didn't *have* to offer me a new contract. But I had broken into the first team, so it made sense for the club to try to protect what was potentially one of its future assets.

Doddsy always tells me a story about Rangers receiving a substantial bid from Leeds United for me, but I don't think the club even told me about it. I can't say that's definitely true, but I don't see why Doddsy would have said it to me.

After a while in the first team, it's fair to say that I had my issues with the money I was on. Walter was the one who had wanted me to sign and I would have hoped that both he and the club could see what I was worth. In hindsight, I should have had an agent and got him to see Walter, who could have then negotiated with the board for the money I was really worth. That original contract, which at the time I didn't question, should have been torn up and replaced by a new deal after a year or two. Most top-class players at Rangers in those days were on great money, certainly compared with me.

Or maybe I should just have gone to Walter, even though he could be a fearsome character, and spoken to him. I could always tell what sort of a mood he was in, so maybe I should have plucked up the courage and just asked for what I thought I deserved for the contribution I was making. Walter was a hard bastard – in a good way – and he did always try to make sure the players were well looked after. I've always regretted not going to him and just asking for the sort of contract other players were on.

Walter's big strength as a boss was how he let the team bond together. He assembled the right group of players who he knew would gel. Then he sat back and watched them grow as a unit. He didn't involve himself too much in the dressing-room. He just let us play. He knew we were good players and he knew he could trust us to do the business for him. He never tried to mollycoddle us or treat us like children. Maybe I was the exception – but I'll get on to that! But, for the most part, he treated the squad the same. He showed us respect and gained ours in return.

He was a first-class man-manager, there's no doubt about that. Walter knew what was required for different games, or different opposition, and he would intervene when he felt he had to. If he felt he needed a reaction, he'd stick a negative press cutting up on the wall of the dressing-room, knowing that it would get our backs up.

It's difficult to explain the dynamic of that dressing-room. The players were actually well-behaved – but absolutely mad at the same time, if that makes any sense. There were no bad apples in there and Walter deserves huge credit for that. It was Walter who fostered that kind of spirit.

Obviously Gazza was completely daft, as everyone knows, but

he was the nicest guy in the world at the same time. Coisty and Durranty were the jokers, along with the Goalie. But Walter was great at getting the right mix of characters. That's how he got the best out of us.

People always ask me about his team-talks but, amazingly, Walter said very little immediately before matches. If fact, most of the time he didn't even come into the dressing-room prior to games. He'd be up in his office at Ibrox, even before Old Firm games or big European ties. You wouldn't see that much of him. Maybe that was part of his aura. Everyone knows that he'd spend the first half of games sitting in the stand and only come down to the dugout area well into the second half.

Archie and Doddsie would be around prior to kick-off. They'd do the warm-up; then at around 2 p.m. Walter would come in, name the team, then disappear again. About ten minutes before the start, he'd come in and say a few words. It wasn't tactical stuff; it was more motivational. And the one thing I would say about Walter Smith is that he had every single player in that changing-room wanting to play for him. No matter what he did to me, or however harshly treated I felt at times, I always had a burning desire to play for the man. He didn't have to deliver huge, inspiring speeches. Those boys were so focused, they barely took in what he actually said. Walter just had a presence about him and he could be an intimidating character. The players wanted to play for him and do well.

You have to understand, that group was full of determined, focused individuals. They liked a carry-on at times, but when it came to game time, they were in the zone. Guys like John Brown, the Goalie, Laudrup, Hateley, McCoist – they all knew what had to be done.

Me? I was just so concentrated on trying to do well in the games. Listen, Ibrox is a difficult place to play, especially for a young kid. You can be playing well, but if the score's still 0–0, the fans get restless and edgy. It's not easy. People think it's a doddle when you're playing for Rangers against the other Scottish clubs because you have the best players and should beat them comfortably, but there's a huge pressure on you when you're wearing that jersey. If you go 1–0 down, it can be a real battle to get a result. But you *have* to, for the supporters. Thankfully we seemed to do quite well in that regard, because we fought back on many occasions to win games.

If you weren't delivering, at half-time Walter would give you your character. You didn't want to get on the wrong side of him and he wouldn't think twice about going through you like a dose of salts if you weren't pulling your weight. But, in many ways, that dressing-room took care of itself, if things weren't going well, with guys like Bomber, Gough, Goram and McCoist in it. If someone wasn't at it, they'd be told in no uncertain terms by the other players more than anyone else, including Walter.

I remember Archie losing it once at half-time in a game against Falkirk when we weren't performing. He booted one of those big kit hampers at full force. It must have been agony, because those containers are rock solid. He actually made a dent in it, but he hid the pain quite well.

Despite all the success we had domestically during my time at Ibrox, the one that I'm sure still rankles with Walter and Archie was how we performed in the Champions League. Even when I think back now, it's strange to me that we didn't do well enough in Europe.

It's only my opinion, but I think the 3-5-2 formation that we played in most Champions League games was a killer for us. Inevitably, it turned into a 5-3-2 with us on the back foot, and it was tough for us against top European sides. You need real quality in the full-back areas to play that formation and, with all due respect, Alex Cleland on the right was more of a steady, traditional type of player for Rangers rather than the more modern wing-back. And Davie Robertson – as good as he was going forward on the left – didn't always get back quickly enough.

Personally, I always felt we should have played with a back four, even it had been 4-5-1, or 4-2-1-3 with Gazza as the one, I'm not sure. But we should have done so much better.

In 2008, when Walter took his second Rangers team to the UEFA Cup final, he was a different manager. He organised that side far more defensively and made them so hard to beat. He set them up not to concede, and it worked for them. He had done the same as Scotland manager previously. He played a grafter up front and got the rest of the team to work their balls off for him. It might not have been pretty to watch, but it was effective.

I would have loved to be part of that squad in 2008, with Walter as gaffer and Coisty as his assistant. It would certainly have been different to his first spell at the club, with Archie as his right-hand man. The pair of them were 'old school', there's no doubt about that. But I also think that, in certain respects, Walter was ahead of his time. He knew the game was changing dramatically in the late '90s. He could sense it and he knew Rangers had to change as well. That's why the likes of Moller Nielsen was introduced. It was also why, after winning nine-in-a-row, that Walter made changes to the squad.

Walter admired Italian football and bought the likes of Sergio Porrini from Juventus, Lorenzo Amoruso from Fiorentina and Marco Negri from Perugia. All three, possibly with the exception of Negri, proved to be terrific signings for Rangers. But, in hindsight, I think those changes probably cost us ten-in-a-row. Walter was right in his thinking – I just feel he did it a year too soon. To go on and win ten-in-a-row, he needed strong characters who knew what it would mean to win that title and beat Celtic's record, which we'd equalled the previous year. It was the wrong time and if Walter had waited twelve months, keeping the nucleus of boys we already had, we'd have won that tenth championship. I'm convinced of it.

Walter was trying to move with the times and I'd never criticise anyone for that. I just think there was too much disruption that season, culminating in his own announcement that he'd be leaving the club at the end of the campaign. By that time, my own relationship with Walter wasn't great. By then, I'd had five years with him and I felt I was an easy target for him. That feeling had been with me from early on in my Rangers career. He'd let certain people away with things that he wouldn't let me away with. It seemed that he'd cut everyone a bit of slack except me!

I was always an easy guy for Walter to drop, and I think that was wrong. I know that, at times, I wasn't the best-behaved player in the world, but I was by no means the worst either. It annoyed me and I often felt that I was made a scapegoat by the gaffer.

At the start of that ten-in-a-row season, I was playing at right wing-back and doing well. I had featured in eight of the first ten games of the campaign, but for the first Old Firm game of the season, in November, I was bombed. Walter didn't even name me on the bench, which was a horrible feeling – even though Goughie scored to give us a 1–0 win at Ibrox.

Arguably, though, the worst moment I had under Walter was a couple of years earlier, when I felt as low as I'd ever been in my career. It was just a little thing to him, but it was massively disappointing for me. He had me in for a dressing-down, for whatever reason, and said, 'Don't ever think you're a Gascoigne or a Laudrup. Just you get the ball and give it to one of them.' For a young player, that kind of comment is like a dagger through the heart. I was devastated, because I suddenly felt that Walter didn't rate me as a player.

Listen, I never for a minute thought I was as good as Paul Gascoigne or Brian Laudrup. Those two were world-class players who have played at the highest level, and are included in the Greatest Ever Rangers Team, which was chosen by Rangers fans. But as a young player still making my way in the game, I wanted to aspire to be as good as them. And I could play. I knew I could play in their company and not look out of place. In fact, I thrived on it. I could see passes others couldn't. But it was difficult just to get the ball in that team because of the quality of player we had. I always thought of myself as very good at set pieces. I had scored free kicks and penalties all through my youth career, but I couldn't get near one at Rangers because the likes of Gazza, Lauders or Albertz were all over them. At corners, it was Gazza's ball, end of story.

At one time during Walter's last season, I was actually getting a game at right wing-back because I could take a long throw-in! If you tried to beat a man and it didn't come off, I'd have senior, experienced players moaning the face off me. That was hard to deal with at times.

So for Walter to say that, it knocked me and knocked my confidence a bit. As I've said, I think I was an easy target.

I was never innocent in Walter's eyes. He always had a reason to bin me from the team or have a pop. There were incidents in which I deliberately didn't get involved but still ended up in trouble. I remember being in the Tunnel nightclub in Glasgow one night. I was inside chatting to one of the bouncers. The next minute, all hell broke loose and fighting erupted. The following morning it was reported in the papers that myself and Derek McInnes were at the heart of it, which was just nonsense, but that was enough for Walter. He got it in his mind that we'd caused a riot on a night out. We had nothing at all to do with it and were completely innocent, but he didn't see it that way. He dragged me into his office the following day and I told him I'd done nothing. 'Aye, you never do fucking anything, do you?' he said. I think I got a fine for that.

On another occasion, we were playing Dunfermline in the semi-final of the 1996/97 League Cup at Celtic Park. We'd normally meet at Ibrox and go for lunch at a hotel in town before travelling to the match, but at around noon I nipped into a bookies on Paisley Road West to have a look at a football coupon for that night. The game wasn't kicking off until 7.45 p.m., remember. It had never been a problem for me before. In fact, it was almost part of my pre-match routine. While I was in there, I saw that a horse I really fancied was just about to run. I was at the counter about to put £200 on the nose when I saw a car pulling up outside. It was the gaffer and Archie. I didn't get the bet or a coupon on before Archie burst in the door. 'Get your arse to the hotel now,' he said. So I drove to the Moat House Hotel, and while I was standing at the lift, Walter came over and said, 'Just you get the fuck up the road, you're not involved tonight.'

I was stunned. Absolutely gutted. It just felt as if he was picking on me. He wouldn't have done that to any of the senior players. So that was me. I'd not only lost £1,000 from that horse I fancied romping in, I'd also missed out on a £6,000 bonus for beating Dunfermline and reaching the League Cup final. That was all for trying to put a football coupon on. On a Saturday, we'd *all* be putting coupons on just three hours before a game and the gaffer didn't seem to bat an eyelid about that.

It was crazy. Listen, maybe Walter thought I was being a wee bastard at times and he was trying to teach me a lesson. But it certainly didn't help me. Perhaps, deep down, he knew that I had real talent and he was on my back to try to get the best out of me. I don't know. I'd have thought there was a better way of doing it. From my viewpoint, he was horrible to me at times.

I'm good friends with the former Rangers defender Michael Ball now, even though we didn't get to play together at Ibrox. Michael was signed by Dick Advocaat for £6 million in 2001 and was a terrific player. Unfortunately, his time at Rangers was seriously hampered by bad injuries. We've been on a few trips to Dubai together for an annual Scotland v England old boys' match. Bally played under Walter and Archie at Everton and according to him they'd often use me as an example to young players at Goodison Park. They'd say things like, 'You don't want to end up like a kid we had at Rangers called Charlie Miller. He had all the talent in the world and had a chance – but wasted it.' Who knows, maybe they told Wayne Rooney not to end up like Charlie Miller!

Seriously, I'm not sure how I feel about that. In a way, I'm pleased that Walter and Archie obviously rated me as a player, but I don't think I did *that* badly in the game, compared with a lot of other talented young players who have the world at their feet early on in their career but never win a trophy or even establish themselves at a big club. I did both.

I still played more than three hundred games for Rangers and I'm proud of that. Is there part of me that wishes I'd have just done everything Walter told me to and never misbehaved? Of course. But I wasn't a bad kid. At times, I just got caught up in things that I wish I hadn't – like the incident at the Fox And Hounds pub, which I'll discuss later. I was a young, gullible guy from Castlemilk who probably didn't realise what I had, but the flipside is that it's difficult for a Glasgow boy to play for Rangers and handle that pressure. I hear players and coaches talking about it all the time now. They talk about how many players fall by the wayside when they go on to play for either of the Old Firm clubs. Better players than me have failed at Rangers or Celtic because they didn't have the mentality to deal with it. I think I did.

That said, never at any point in my Rangers career can I recall Walter putting his arm around me and saying, 'Look, Charlie, you have to buck up your ideas.' He did that for Gazza at times. He sympathised with him, but with me he clearly thought a boot up the arse was more beneficial. I probably needed the arm round the shoulder at times and Walter just didn't realise it.

People ask if I wish Walter had been more of a father figure to me in my life. And I suppose, yeah, I'd have liked him to treat me more like he did the other boys in the Rangers team. I have never known my dad and, as I've already said, I had my uncles, Benny and Jim, who took over that role. They were great. But I signed for a club the size of Rangers and was in the first team at seventeen. I didn't really know how to deal with that at that time. It was totally new and I didn't realise what I had. Maybe Walter could have helped me more.

When I see Walter now, we're fine. I met him in the summer of 2013 when I was coming back from Hong Kong, where I play every year for the Rangers all-star team. We bumped into each other at the airport and there will never be a problem between myself and Walter. To him, I'm still just 'wee Charlie' and that's fine. That will never change. I'll always be 'young Chico', the young upstart – the baby of the family, if you like.

Despite everything I've said about him, I take my share of responsibility too. I wasn't perfect, far from it. I've said elsewhere in these pages that I took my eye off the ball at Rangers for a spell and, ultimately, I paid for it. At times, I admit that I was more interested in where we were going for a drink after the game than I was on the match itself. I know now how wrong that was and I regret it.

Also, I have to say that Walter was very approachable when I was a bit short of money. At times when I wasn't playing and money was a bit tight, I could go to him and he'd try to help me out. If I ever had a problem at home or with the family, I felt I could go to him for advice, so that was good. During those periods, I was very grateful to him and I'll never forget that.

He's still the best manager I ever worked under – and I had a few after I left Rangers in 1999. I had spells at Leicester (on loan), Watford, Dundee United, Brann Bergen, Lierse, Brisbane Roar, Gold Coast United and Clyde.

And along the way, I've worked with some top-class coaches, like Martin O'Neill, a great guy who I'd have liked to play under for longer. You never saw him on the training ground that much at Leicester; it was John Robertson and Steve Walford who did the coaching. I was only there for a few months but I really liked the three of them and I enjoyed working with them. Even in later years, when I played for Dundee United against their Celtic side, they would make a point of coming to speak to me. Martin was quite similar to Walter in a lot of ways. He was a motivator and he got a squad together who he knew he could trust. All the boys believed in him. That summed up Martin – he had a team who were all desperate to play for him. He was good for them and they were good for him. I didn't have a problem with him and I knew when he joined Celtic in 2000 that he'd do well. Even after just a few months on loan at Filbert Street, I was convinced he'd be a huge success at Parkhead. He's a strong man who has a presence about him. You wouldn't mess with Martin. He is an eloquent speaker but he didn't waste words. And, make no mistake, he had big characters in his dressing-room both at Leicester and Celtic. At Filbert Street when I was there, you had Steve Walsh, Matt Elliott, Gerry Taggart, Muzzy Izzet, Robbie Savage, Neil Lennon, Frank Sinclair, Steve Guppy, Emile Heskey and Tony Cottee. Even the foreign boys like Kasey Keller, the USA keeper, and the Greek captain Theo Zagorakis were great lads.

The two people most people ask me about are Lenny, for obvious reasons, and Savage. They were both terrific lads and excellent players. Robbie would cover every blade of grass and Lenny wouldn't. Lenny just kept things simple: that was his style and he was brilliant at it.

In my first start for Leicester, I got injured against Newcastle. We won 2–0, but I was taken off after a tackle from Gary Speed. It wasn't a nasty challenge and it's a tragedy that Gary isn't with us now. But he tackled me, I picked up a bad injury and that was me out for the rest of that 1998/99 season. I only played in a handful of games, which was a real shame, because I feel if I'd have stayed fit and played more, I could have made a real impact at Leicester.

I remember shortly after I arrived I scored four goals in one reserve game. It was a good experience. They put me up at the Stakis Hotel in Leicester, which was my first spell away from Glasgow in my football life. But I relished it and I was eager to impress. I've always thought of myself as a personable guy and fairly well liked, so it wasn't difficult for me to settle at Leicester and it's a regret of mine that I didn't work more under Martin.

When I left Rangers for good in 1999, I opted to join Watford and hook up with a former England manager. But the problem with Graham Taylor was that it was all about Graham Taylor. I'm not saying he was necessarily a bad person. He was, in my opinion, just a really bad manager, as I think he'd proved previously when he had that disastrous spell as England boss.

Everything was about him. He'd get the team in on a Saturday morning at 9 a.m., do a 'loosener' with them and then speak to them for a full hour in a team meeting. After that, we'd go back to the hotel to get a pre-match meal before heading back to the stadium. You just don't do that – but Graham did. It was unreal, absolute madness.

Graham made Watford at that time a club full of cliques – I think that was his doing. I remember he told myself, Neil Cox, Nordin Wooter and Des Lyttle to leave the dressing-room one day because he wanted to have a team meeting – but only with the boys who'd been at the club the previous year! That was one of the strangest things I'd ever heard in all my time in football. He dropped the three of us all at once as well.

When I signed for Watford, I had the option of going to Charlton instead. But, initially, Graham impressed me. He's a decent guy, not a bad person at all. And I wanted to play for him. But I just don't think he's a very good manager – the same as he'll probably say I wasn't that good a footballer.

I should never have signed there. Only now, when I look back, I say to myself 'What were you doing?' I was going from a club of Rangers' size and stature to Watford, who paled in comparison. The set-up was poor, even though they were in the Premier League. I think they'd reached the top flight too soon and we went straight back down again, despite beating Chelsea at home and Liverpool at Anfield that season.

I left in November 2000 for Dundee United, and by that time I was desperate to get out of the place. After being relegated, they were pissing the Championship – absolutely flying. But Graham absolutely murdered the squad fitness-wise. The training he had the boys doing was relentless. He'd run them into the ground during the week, despite the fact they were playing three games in seven days in the Championship. It was just ridiculous. It was run, run, run. He killed them, and by Christmas, the players were gone. If he hadn't done that, I'm convinced they'd have gone back up again.

I didn't play a single game in the Championship after Graham completely bombed me out, yet he'd take me to every fucking away match we played in. Honestly, I must have visited every ground in the league that season without getting my Watford tracksuit off.

It wasn't a glamorous side at Watford; it wasn't packed full of big names. The Scottish striker Allan Smart was there and he scored our winner against Chelsea. And it was Tommy Mooney who grabbed the glory at Anfield against Liverpool. The likes of Cox, Wooter and big Robert Page, who skippered Wales, were the most well-known players in the squad, but they were a good team together.

One of the good things Graham did do was sign Espen Baardsen and Allan Nielsen from Spurs. They were great lads and top players and both of them did really well for Watford. But I had to get out of there and get back home. I was angling for a move back to Scotland and, thankfully, Dundee United came in for me.

Alex Smith was my manager there and I loved him to bits. He liked me, I liked him, and I still think Alex was hard done by at Tannadice. He'd already been harshly treated at Aberdeen years previously when he took them to within a game of the title and won both the League Cup and Scottish Cup, but was still sacked. That was a disgrace. Wee Alex may have been 'old school' in some of his methods, but he wanted you to play and, more importantly, he wanted to give young players a chance.

He'd just taken over at United shortly before I arrived. I was one of his first signings and the club were in a bad situation near the bottom of the SPL table. I remember I signed on the Thursday, trained on the Friday and played against Motherwell at Fir Park on the Saturday. I hadn't played in over six months, but Alex threw me in.

It was strange – and I'm not trying to blow my own trumpet – but after that match, Alex's long-time assistant John Blackley came into the dressing-room and said to me, 'I didn't realise how good a player you really are.' It was a weird thing for a manager or coach to say, but I had been out of the picture for so long – maybe a lot of people in Scotland at that time had forgotten about me. At first I thought, 'Cheeky old bastard,' before I realised he was paying me a big compliment.

On my travels around the globe, three gaffers stick out who, one way or another, had a big influence on me. The first was Mons Ivar Mjelde, who was my coach at Brann, in Norway. He was a Norwegian international as a player and he's still coaching there now as manager of Start. Mjelde trained us like bears when I was at Brann and he just didn't fancy me as a player. It wasn't him who signed me from Dundee United; it was the club's director of football, Per-Ove Ludvigsen.

The fans loved me in Bergen, but Mjelde wasn't having me at all. I'd score a goal in the 50th minute to put us in front in a game – then on fifty-five minutes, he'd take me off! I remember once, when we were on a bad run, I told him he had to change the side. He was sticking with the same guys every week, who weren't playing well at all. After I'd spoken to him, he said, 'You're right, Charlie,' and duly dropped *me*. He then told the local press that I didn't want to play, which was rubbish.

There was also a game against Stabaek that is lodged in my mind. Robbie Winters, my fellow Scot, had scored to put us one up. There were only six minutes to go and Mjelde was getting someone else stripped to come on from the bench. But Stabaek then scored to make it 1–1 and suddenly he needed me. I went on and hit a 90th-minute winner.

What a strike it was – one touch with my right foot and bang into the far corner of the net. Mjelde was going wild, celebrating with us. But all I could think of was 'you bastard' – he'd left me out and then I saved his skin.

At half-time in a game against FC Lyn, we were losing 1–0 and Mjelde, his assistant and the captain Martin Andreson spent the entire fifteen minutes in a wee treatment room, not saying a single word to the team. When they came out, I lost it. I was raging. I was shouting, 'What the fuck is going on?' We were losing 1–0 and they weren't even giving us any instructions. But it was too late – half-time was over, they sent us back out and we lost the game. Very strange.

Another foreign boss I worked under was Kjetil Rekdal at Lierse, in Belgium. While I was in Norway at Brann, he was manager of Vålerenga and had been impressed by me. That's why he took me to Lierse. I remember, shortly after signing, I injured my thigh and had to have an injection. The physio at Lierse told him to leave me out, but Rekdal asked me if I could play and I said yes. The physio was very angry and said, 'He shouldn't play.' But Rekdal said, 'He's playing – even injured, he's still better than what we've got.' I loved that.

The boys at Lierse hated him, but I liked Rekdal. There's a big thing in Belgium about everyone shaking each other's hand when they meet, including every day in the workplace, but Rekdal didn't give a fuck and completely ignored the ritual from the minute he arrived. I liked his little bit of arrogance and he eventually got a great move, going to coach Kaiserslautern in Germany.

Finally, I have to mention my old coach in Australia, Frank Farina, who I worked with at Brisbane Roar. I've said elsewhere in the book that, aside from Walter, Farina was the best I ever played for. He's a great man-manager and I still respect him a lot. He got together a squad at Brisbane who played really well together – and got on like a house on fire. He was like Walter, in that sense. We had myself, Craig Moore, ex-Manchester City midfielder Danny Tiatto and wee Matt McKay to name a few. Matt was a terrific player, despite not hitting it off at Rangers a few years ago. Farina signed good players from abroad as well, like Sergio van Dijk from Holland. Incredibly, Sergio had a bigger arse than me but he was still a cracking player! Frank was brilliant. He's also managed the Socceroos, Australia's national team, and he's someone I always want to see do well.

As you'll discover later, though, I still regard Walter as the best manager I ever worked with. He *has* to be. His achievements, at Rangers in particular, were outstanding. And if he hadn't given me my chance in one of the club's greatest-ever sides, my football career might have ended before it had begun.

6

NINE-IN-A-ROW

IT'S a question I'm often asked: when did it actually sink in that I'd played my part in winning nine-in-a-row for Rangers? Was it when I crossed the ball for Brian Laudrup to head home the winning goal against Dundee United to clinch the title? Was it when the referee blew for full-time at Tannadice and the fans went wild in celebration at finally equalling Celtic's forty-year-old record? Or was it watching our skipper Richard Gough lift the trophy for the ninth successive time in floods of tears at creating history for the club?

Honestly? The magnitude of the achievement in 1997 only hit me when I saw seasoned England internationals Mark Hateley and Trevor Steven downing alcoholic shots at Reds nightclub in Glasgow after we'd got back from Dundee. That might sound daft but it's true. Until that point, I hadn't really felt the pressure of trying to win nine-in-a-row. I was still young, a bit wet behind the ears. To me, it was just another league championship for Rangers. But that night, when a large chunk of the squad went to Reds for a celebratory party, it hit me.

I remember sitting in the corner, just me, Oz and Del McInnes, having a few pints. Suddenly it dawned on me what we'd done. And a huge weight seemed to lift off my shoulders. So I *must* have felt some pressure during that season for me to feel like that.

But the key moment was watching guys like Mark and Trevor at the bar. I could just see the sheer joy, happiness and – most important – relief etched on their faces. These were boys who hadn't grown up as Rangers fans, but they'd taken the club to their hearts and had bought into the whole nine-in-a-row crusade. It meant so much to them to win that ninth title. Obviously, it meant even more to the likes of Coisty, Durranty, the Goalie, Bomber, Goughie and Fergie, who'd been there through so many title wins. But the size of the achievement only became clear to me that night at Reds. I had played in seven-in-a-row and eight-in-a-row – and now I had made a major contribution to the magical nine.

In that seven-in-a-row season, 1994/95, I wasn't even aware of how important it was to chase the nine. For me it was just about playing games for Rangers, I hadn't really looked beyond that. It wasn't as if I was saying, 'We're getting closer to nine-in-a-row,' even though I know the fans would have been. But from a selfish point of view, it was all about establishing myself in the first team.

In the summer of 1994, ahead of the seven-in-a-row season, there was the incident in Castlemilk that saw me interviewed as part of a murder investigation, so I wasn't sure what lay ahead that year. I wasn't even sure if I was going to play any more games for the club after making my debut the previous season and feeling as if I'd let myself down with my performance – I was determined not to let that happen again. I think Walter was just relieved that I hadn't been around the scene of the murder and wasn't directly involved in what happened that night. The police no longer wanted to talk to me, so that went in my favour with Walter. I knew that if I started the season well, I'd have a chance. And I got my first game on 1 October, against Dundee United at Ibrox when Lauders scored his first goal for Rangers with a stunning run and finish. Before that, I was beginning to think Walter had doubts about me. I was worried that he might not think I was good enough to make the step up, but he threw me in against

United. I was up against Billy McKinlay in midfield and played really well that day. We won 2–0 and I stayed in the team.

Laudrup was special. I knew he'd be a superstar at Rangers from the minute he walked in the door. I loved playing with him. And, although I'm not saying I was anywhere near as good as Lauders, I think that when it came to certain things like when to make a pass or the timing of a run, we were on the same wavelength. I'd like to think he enjoyed playing with me.

Michael Mols, who played for Rangers years later, had this special wee turn that the fans loved, but Brian had it long before him. Every time Lauders turned, I felt as if he was going to badly twist his knee or that the defender he was up against would. He had the longest body in the world, but the shortest legs. He was a great guy to have in the dressing-room. He didn't act like a superstar, even though he was one. Nobody at Rangers did back then – you would quickly get cut down to size if you did. But he was in a different class.

It probably worked out well for me that Brian's form at Rangers actually started to pick up when I got into the team. At the start of that seven-in-a-row season, the boys had lost three crucial games in the space of a week against Celtic in the league, AEK Athens in the Champions League qualifier and Falkirk in the League Cup. It was a disastrous seven days for Walter and the club, especially, as he'd signed Brian and ex-Champions League winner Basile Boli during the summer. The mood around the place was horrendous and the boys were really down.

People might think it was the ideal time for me to come in, but it wasn't – because the pressure was on the team after those three results. But Laudrup started to motor after that United game and the fans were buzzing again fairly quickly, because they realised what a player they had on their hands. They were also delighted that I was in the team, a young Glasgow boy who had come through the ranks, so all of a sudden the gloom was lifting and everyone was in good spirits again.

Everyone knows about the camaraderie we had in the dressing-room back then. It was a special group of players. And yet our training conditions were a nightmare: firstly at the Albion, then afterwards when we had to drive all over Glasgow for a pitch. I'm not saying I was the best trainer in the world, but I'd like to think if I had the kind of facilities players have now at Murray Park, I'd have stayed late some days to practise. There's everything there for you at Murray Park. It would have improved everyone in our squad if we'd had that at our disposal.

I won't lie: I hated running in training or doing weights. But I loved the football side of it. Back then, we'd turn up at Ibrox, get changed and be on the bus for 10 a.m. None of us knew where we'd be going on any specific day. One morning it would be Partick, the next Jordanhill, and the following day we'd be at a cricket club. We had one training pitch near Gartnavel Hospital, which we used to call the San Siro. Obviously, it was an ironic nickname because it was one of the worst pitches you could ever play football on.

But McCoist, in particular, was brilliant in terms of cheering everyone up. He'd turn up almost every morning just five minutes before we were due to leave for training. We'd all be on the minibus, on the track inside Ibrox, ready to go and waiting on Coisty. Jimmy Bell, the kit man and driver, would jump in and drive round to the front door of the stadium. Sure enough, Coisty would be there after a thirty-second change of clothes, with a newspaper, a cup of tea and a bacon roll. We'd all shout: 'Leave that fat bastard here!' But wee Jimmy never would. Then we'd be up the back of the bus pelting Coisty with things – but he'd go through the exact same routine the following day.

It was an enjoyable time for me and I could feel a reaction to me from the punters. The last boy to come through before me was Sandy Robertson in the early '90s, but he didn't play too many times in the first team. I didn't think I'd made it after that United game, but I felt good. Unlike my debut at Pittodrie, for instance, I felt I had done myself justice and deserved to retain my place.

I played in eighteen of the next twenty league games for Rangers, which included two Old Firm games against Celtic. One was my first at Hampden, where I teed up big Mark for his goal in that brilliant 3–1 victory. And the other was on 4 January 1995, which ended 1–1, with Ian Ferguson getting our goal. I should actually have scored myself just before Fergie got on the end of it, but Celtic defender Tam Boyd came right through the back of me as I was about to shoot. He kneed me in the back and I had to go off injured at half-time.

I think Tam thought, 'I'm not letting this wee bastard score' – after I'd robbed him of the ball at Hampden in the previous game in the build-up to Mark's goal. He meant it and was always incredibly competitive. Tam wasn't dirty, but he wanted to let me know I wouldn't get the better of him again.

I actually played as a striker for Rangers that night, but I don't think I ever really played well up front. I didn't enjoy it. But I had twenty-one starts that season and scored three goals, which wasn't a bad return for a nineteen-year-old.

As well as Lauders, we also had guys like Stuart McCall, who was a tiger in the middle of the park for us. He might not have produced defence-splitting passes, but the wee man could play. I liked Stuart a lot. He never made me feel that I shouldn't be playing next to him. Sometimes, older, experienced guys might look down on a young kid in the team and make him feel as if he doesn't deserve to be in that company, but Stuart wasn't like that – even though he had over fifty caps for Scotland at the time. He just expected me to play and he knew I was good enough. That's the way it was at Rangers. If you played in the first team, you were just expected to go out and do the business in every game you played. Yet even then, I never fully felt like a first-team player. For example, I still wasn't changing in the first-team dressing-room at this point. I just wasn't comfortable doing that yet.

Walter didn't really say much to me that season. It wasn't as if he was in my ear all the time giving me advice and telling me what to do. He treated me like a Rangers first-team player and as long as I was performing for him on the park – and behaving off it – he was great with me.

Another thing people always ask me is which players in that changing-room particularly helped me. But it wasn't about that. The most important thing was that they accepted me. They didn't have to help me settle in. I didn't think I was a 'Jack the Lad', but I had a bit of banter and I felt at ease with them on and off the pitch. I gave as good as I got in the banter department. I wouldn't say any of the boys in particular made me a better player. None of them ever advised me or sat me down to give me pointers. Maybe it's because they knew I could play.

That said, looking back, I have one regret about when I first properly broke into that Rangers team: I became too passive in games. Instead of beating a man and shooting for goal, I'd tend to beat a man and then square it to a team-mate. I had played against top players at reserve level for Rangers, but when I got to the first team I started to worry about what other people were saying or thinking about me – and I shouldn't have. It still irks me to this day that I wasn't more confident on the pitch when I was younger. In the reserves, I was running the show, creating and scoring goals, but I was a different player a lot of the time in the first team. Moaning faces like Gazza, Coisty and Hateley, who would be raging if you didn't square the ball to them, might not have helped, right enough.

My first goal for Rangers was against Kilmarnock on 15 October. Big Mark headed it down to me in the box, I took a touch, spun, and banged it in. It was actually a big goal, because it was 0–0 at the time. I remember there was a real sense of relief around the ground when I scored. The fans were desperate for a goal that day.

Again, it's probably only now when I look back that I realise how important a goal like that was, in terms of us going on to win the seventh title. It didn't sink in back then. It was in the 78th minute against Killie, who were a horrible team to play against. We always struggled against them. Thankfully, after I'd scored, Davie Roberson clinched the win with a late goal.

I scored another winner in that season, an early goal against Hearts at Ibrox in January. That was one of the worst football games I've ever been involved in. It was a great ball from Lauders through the middle of the Hearts defence; I took a touch, gave their keeper, Craig Nelson, the eyes and put it in the opposite corner.

By that time at Ibrox, I was involved in the 'Tuesday Club'. A few of the lads would go out for a 'bonding session' every Tuesday, because Wednesday was our day off. We'd go to Buzzy Wares in Princes Square quite often, or Vroni's on West Nile Street for lunch. We went to loads of different places in Glasgow city centre. I remember one day in particular they took me to Ho Wong, a Chinese restaurant on York Street. The food was absolutely beautiful, but unfortunately so was the bevvy, and I couldn't handle my drink. I think I was slung in a taxi about 7 p.m., steaming.

The Tuesday regulars were the usual crowd: McCoist, Doddsie, Oz, McCall, Durrant and the Goalie. The Steps Bar was a regular haunt, because we could get a bet in there as well. No one bothered you in the Steps, which was great. That type of thing just wouldn't happen now. Can you imagine five or six players from Rangers or Celtic going out on a Tuesday afternoon to the West End of Glasgow and having a few beers and a punt? It just wouldn't happen. It would be all over social media within minutes. There would be pictures, videos, the lot – and that would be it finished.

The Steps Bar is an old man's pub and all the guys in there knew we'd be in on a Tuesday, so they wouldn't bother you. Players wouldn't go to a boozer like that now, but we loved it. The regulars were quite protective of us. There would even be a few Celtic fans in there as well, but they wouldn't give us an ounce of hassle.

We used to have some laughs, but I was still a major lightweight when it came to the bevvy. I'd have five or six pints and I was away with it. We'd have Wednesday off and I'd go for a few cans that day with my pals Rab and Lenny. That was my day to go back up to Castlemilk and see my mates. The drink wasn't really bothering me at that stage, because I was training hard almost every day and I was fit as fuck.

Winning that first title was special in 1994/95. So was picking up the SPFA Young Player of the Year award for that season. That was a proud moment for me, especially with Lauders winning the Player of the Year trophy. In truth, I probably expected to win it. There weren't many good young Scottish kids coming through at that time. Simon Donnelly and Jackie McNamara were probably my only challengers.

I had to make a speech at the SPFA dinner and I was still only nineteen. Walter's advice to me was: 'Don't you fucking be drunk when you go up there.' I had to stay sober before saying a few words. Thankfully, I've kept all my medals and trophies, and they're looked after by a relative.

My problem at that time was that I thought I'd just win more and more throughout my career. It was the norm at Rangers. Celtic weren't even getting close to us at that point – Motherwell even finished above them that season. I felt proud that I'd won it. That was my first major medal and I could look at it and actually feel that I'd contributed to it. I felt comfortable in that team. I'd played over twenty games, so it wasn't as if I'd just played a couple and then been left out again.

My profile had probably changed, but I still naively didn't think anyone knew me. I didn't do many media interviews at the time, but I remember doing one with Jim White for STV. I wasn't very confident in front of the cameras and wasn't overly keen on doing it. I still cringe to this day about it. STV were trying to promote this image of me as a cheeky wee Glasgow guy. So Jim put me on the spot and said, 'Right, when the camera rolls, slag me. Just think of something and have a wee joke at my expense.'

I didn't know what to say. I just froze. When the camera went on I laughed and said, 'Look at your hair, it's just a cloud of grey.' What does that even mean? It was the worst joke ever and I can't believe I said it. It didn't do much for my reputation!

We eventually won the league with a 3–1 victory over Hibs at Ibrox in mid-April. Darren Jackson put them ahead in the first half, but we responded well and goals from Jukey, Durranty and Alexei Mikhailichenko got us over the line.

The saddest time of that season was the tragic death of Davie Cooper, who died of a brain haemorrhage on 23 March 1995. I didn't know Davie at all until one day I was invited along to Ayr Racecourse for the day with him, Coisty and big Derek Johnstone. It was only about a month before Davie died. It was a brilliant day and I loved Davie's dry sense of humour. I remember Coisty and D.J. talking about me and saying to him, 'The wee man likes a drink.' Coop replied, 'Well, he's got a right good chance of being a player then.'

Little did he know that was probably my downfall! But he picked five out of six winners that day at Ayr and I got none. Davie liked a punt.

He was terrific company and I'll always cherish that memory of him. When he died, I was really sad, especially because I'd only met the man a matter of weeks before. In that one afternoon, I quickly realised why the likes of Coisty and Durranty had always spoken so highly of him, and not just for his brilliance on the pitch. He was taken from us far too soon at the age of just thirty-nine. Understandably, Coisty and Durranty were devastated when he died. It was a tragedy and the Rangers fans were in a state of mourning. They had a shrine to Davie on the gates at Ibrox. He'll certainly never be forgotten.

That pre-season, I went to Australia and Hong Kong with a few of the lads and it was an unforgettable trip. I was there with Oz, Bomber and Archie, among others, and that was when the bevvy started to take its toll on me. This is funny now, but it wasn't at the time. I got so pished one night that I fell asleep. I was out for the count, so Bomber and Archie decided to put me on a *boat* – the one that sails back and forth to Macau, which is a sixty-minute crossing. God knows how many times I must have made that trip, absolutely wrecked, while they carried on drinking. Eventually, they took pity on me and pulled me off it.

We went there for two weeks after winning seven-in-a-row. I must have gone out there weighing about sixty kilos and came back hitting eighty. I was beginning to feel it. I'd come straight back from there to go on holiday with Caroline, my mate Brendan and his missus to Tenerife. That was a week of madness as well. You always kid yourself on as a young player, saying, 'It's fine, I'll come back and do a wee bit before going into pre-season training.' But I never did. I had always been fit for pre-season, but that was the first time I thought, 'Fuck, I'm really feeling it here.'

That summer, 1995/96, was all about Gazza's arrival in Scottish football. All the Rangers boys thought he'd be a brilliant signing and obviously that proved to be the case. At first, I wasn't worried that he'd take my place in midfield. I started the first four league games of the campaign, so I wasn't too concerned. During that spell, Walter also picked me for the League Cup quarter-final tie against Celtic at Parkhead, and I had a hand in Coisty's winning goal. I played the ball to Gazza, who crossed for Coisty and, well, the rest is history.

That was the first game at the 'new' Celtic Park, and Ally took great delight in celebrating in front of the old jungle that night. I was the first guy on his back as he wheeled away. But after a 1–0 defeat to Hibs at Easter Road in the league, I was out of the side for the league game against our main rivals on 30 September.

Alex Cleland somehow managed to score to put us 1–0 up, then Gazza raced clear after Coisty put him in to seal the points and get his first Old Firm goal. At that point, I was worried and thought, 'I'm going to struggle to get a game here.' And I was right. Despite a couple of sub appearances, I didn't start another game until 25 November. I wondered if it was my fitness. Maybe Walter had noticed that the summer exertions had taken the edge off me.

I didn't get back into the side until a 4–1 victory over Hibs, and after that I got a sustained run in the team. Of the next sixteen games, I started thirteen of them, including a 0–0 draw against Celtic at Parkhead. I had made seventeen starts and scored three goals before the infamous 'Fox and Hounds' incident in March, which got me into bother. Then that was me binned for the rest of the season.

It was just four days after the Dunblane massacre that shocked the whole of Scotland to its core. No one will ever forget that tragedy – the like of which had never been seen before in this country. It was worldwide news and it felt unbelievable that something like that could happen here. As the tragic personal stories from that day unfolded, no words could describe the unbearable pain that people who lost family were suffering.

But, somehow, we all had to carry on, and for Rangers that meant an Old Firm game on 17 March – St Patrick's Day – at Ibrox. It was the day before my twentieth birthday, in 1996, and I had been playing a major role in Rangers' charge towards eight-in-a-row.

The game finished 1–1. Big Alan McLaren put us a goal up with a header, but John Hughes equalised with four minutes left to earn Celtic a point. There was the usual wall of noise and terrific atmosphere during the game, as there always was against Celtic, but there was a poignant minute's silence before the match in honour of the kids who lost their lives at Dunblane Primary School on 13 March. Every player, including myself, wore a black armband during the game.

Afterwards, a lot of the players had agreed we were going out.

We were going to the Fox and Hounds pub and restaurant in a wee place called Houston, just outside Glasgow. A crowd of my mates were joining me for a birthday celebration and a squad of Gazza's pals had made the journey up from Gateshead for the game. Jimmy Five Bellies was there, among others.

Gazza himself had gone upstairs in the Fox and Hounds along with the likes of Coisty and some other players. But I didn't want to eat. I just wanted a drink and stayed downstairs with big Oz, my mates and the crowd of Geordies. We were all having a good laugh. Sure, there was a bit of shouting and bawling, but it was all good-natured stuff. There was a lively atmosphere in the place.

It was still early in the evening when a guy – who I now know to be Celtic fan John McKee – walked into the bar with a friend of his and two women. His entrance didn't even register with us, as we were just having a carry-on. Everyone in our wee 'party' over at an alcove in the pub was in high spirits.

But not long after he came in, I watched McKee go up to the manager of the Fox and Hounds and it was clear that he was making some sort of complaint about us. He didn't seem too happy about the way we were enjoying ourselves. I was surprised, because the place was buzzing. It had been a draw at Ibrox, so nothing should have been a problem. There had been no aggro at all up until that point. But I thought from the word go that this guy could be trouble. It later emerged in court that McKee had previous convictions for assault and breach of the peace himself. So he had a bit of history.

I reckon that the manager of the Fox and Hounds effectively told him that if he had a problem, he should leave. But McKee was having none of it. He walked straight over to me, bold as brass, and stood next to my mates and the Geordie boys. Gazza was still upstairs. I wasn't drunk yet, as it was still early in the evening.

At this time, I had been growing this wee stupid goatee beard and McKee grabbed the bottom bit of it. At the same time, he pulled up his sleeve to show me the tattoo he had on his arm. It was a picture of the Pope and an Irish tricolour. He admitted doing this at the subsequent trial.

During our 'exchange', he called me an 'Orange bastard'. Jimmy backed me up on that in court, as was reported in the *Daily Record* and other newspapers at the time. It was a big story and I was on the front pages, as opposed to the back. Jimmy had heard him say it.

I was in total shock, but my mates were ready to go for him. As McKee walked away, I told them to leave it. He wasn't worth it. Those Geordie boys were having to be held back, though. They wanted to sort him out.

Out the corner of my eye, I then saw him and Jimmy getting into an altercation at the bar. Now, Jimmy couldn't fight sleep. He had a heart of gold, but he wasn't a fighter. I was the first one to clock this and I just lost it and flew for McKee. I had put up with the beard pulling and the tattoo, but he was now having a go at a mate and, as far as I could see, Jimmy hadn't done anything wrong.

Big Oz was trying to drag me off him. He was shouting at me, 'What you doing, you daft c***?' Oz was a lot more sensible than me – he could probably see the potential ramifications a mile off. But by this stage the Geordie boys, along with my mates, had got hold of McKee and gave him a real doing. Thankfully, my mate Brains got me the fuck out of there. It was an incident that shouldn't have happened and, of course, I shouldn't have reacted the way I did.

McKee then went to the papers the next day, and his side of the story was laughable. According to him, he'd come over to us in the pub and asked us to stop singing sectarian songs.

In court, he claimed I'd called him a 'Fenian bastard', which I still deny. He also told the court he'd said, 'You were wearing a black armband out of respect for Dunblane today – where's your respect now?' He then stated that my reply was, 'Fuck Dunblane and fuck you.' It was absolute nonsense. As if I'd say that. As a father myself, why would I say something as disgusting as that to a guy I'd never met in my life before?

I immediately had to do a piece in the *Sun* newspaper, completely denying his claims. It was ridiculous. I'm not saying that there weren't a few Rangers songs being sung in the pub that night, but I wouldn't say it was anything too outrageous. It wasn't our fans singing to Celtic fans or vice versa. It was all good-natured banter between us and all of Gazza's Geordie pals. Do you think if there had been seriously offensive sectarian songs being sung that the management and everyone else inside the pub would have stood for it? Not a chance.

There was no sectarianism. We were winding the Geordie boys up and they were doing the same to us. It's as simple as that. It was rowdy, but nothing more, before McKee decided to get involved. He was a Celtic fan who clearly took umbrage to so many Rangers supporters having a good time in his local boozer.

I don't have a problem with Celtic fans. Lots of my mates are huge Celtic supporters. And as I've said earlier, I went to watch Celtic as a kid with my uncle Benny. On another night out with my mates, it might have been a crowd of Celtic boys I was standing with in the pub. But McKee was adamant that he wanted me and others punished for what had happened that night, so he went to the police.

Thankfully, the judge found his evidence less than convincing and I was acquitted of the assault charge and found not proven on breach of the peace. The sheriff, Bill Dunlop, stated that McKee bore 'some considerable responsibility' for what happened in the pub that night. I think that says it all.

The Fox and Hounds incident and what happened afterwards wasn't directly as a result of drinking too much. But if I hadn't been out bevvying after the Old Firm game, I wouldn't have put myself in that position. And that's my problem. I've always liked a night out with my mates and have found it difficult to say no.

Overall, the eight-in-a-row season felt like a let-down for me. It was a fantastic campaign for Rangers – and Gazza especially – and we'd beaten Celtic to the title, even though they'd lost just one game all year. I'd played in a fair amount of games but nowhere near enough, as far as I was concerned. Maybe I'm being a bit hard on myself, but I don't think so.

Because of the Fox and Hounds blot on my copybook, I missed out on the vital last two months of the season. I didn't get involved in the celebrations when Gazza scored his unbelievable hat-trick to beat Aberdeen 3–1 to clinch it. I was in the stand and just didn't feel like celebrating. I don't understand boys who are out on the pitch jumping about after a big win when they haven't kicked a ball for three months.

It also meant that I was left out of the Scottish Cup semi-final victory over Celtic at Hampden and the squad for the final against Hearts in May. That was Lauders' day, as he scored two and teed up Jukey for a treble in a superb 5–1 victory.

Missing those two games was hard to take. I had been bombed for the most pivotal part of the campaign, when all the big games were being played. And all because of a stupid incident in a pub.

Yet that eight-in-a-row season also gave me my first taste of European football for Rangers.

I was on the bench for the Champions League qualifier first leg against Anorthosis Famagusta, largely due to a shin splint problem that was nagging at me. But I was picked for the crucial second leg in the searing heat of Cyprus and I completed ninety minutes. That was yet another vital game that I'm proud to have played my part in, not least because the bonus per man that night was £30,000 if we made it through to the group phase. I was really pleased with my performance: I had two cracking shots – one that the keeper tipped over and one that flew just off target.

So we'd made it to the money-spinning Champions League and we could barely have picked a tougher draw after we were paired with Juventus, Borussia Dortmund and Steaua Bucharest.

I started both games against Borussia Dortmund, which both ended 2–2, and I was picked for the home game against Juve – when we were thumped 4–0 – and the away game in Romania when a late Daniel Prodan goal robbed us of a point. I also came off the bench against Steaua at home when Gazza scored after one of his trademark solo runs from the halfway line, but sadly they salvaged a 1–1 draw.

The only match I didn't play in was in Turin against the Italian champions, who beat us 4–1 over there. Juve were some team at that time. In the game at Ibrox, we actually matched them for forty minutes before Alessandro Del Piero scored. The Goalie had to go off injured at half-time to be replaced by Billy Thomson and Juve stepped it up a gear after the break. They had superstars like Moreno Torricelli, Del Piero and Fabrizio Ravanelli playing for them at that time and they were too good for us.

My most memorable games were the ones against the Germans. I played well in both – and I was up against some world-class midfielders. Dortmund boasted talent like Andreas Möller, Michael Zorc, Karl-Heinz Riedle, Matthias Sammer and Lars Ricken in their line-up, so I was in illustrious company, but I felt I handled myself well. I set up Jukey's goal at the Westfalenstadion and did well alongside Gazza in both games. Unfortunately, just three points in the group was nowhere near good enough to qualify. But on a personal level, the European games *were* something I was proud of that season.

So the eighth title was in the bag. But could we do the nine? That was the question on everyone's lips. I have to confess that I never really felt the pressure. People will find that hard to believe, but the only time I felt it was after we clinched it at Dundee United and we ended up in Reds nightclub. Whether it was because I was young, naive or I hadn't been at the club long enough, I don't know, but I didn't feel the same level of pressure as the older boys who had been through almost every year of the nine.

Listen, I don't doubt that the other boys felt under major

pressure. They were definitely feeling it. Imagine if the likes of McCoist, Durrant, Goram, Gough and Ferguson – who had played in every single championship – *didn't* get the ninth? So they felt it. But I was still a kid and they probably tried to keep that pressure away from me.

From a playing point of view, I have to say that it was a disappointing season for me, simply because I didn't play as many games as I would have liked. Before that night at Tannadice, I had started just six league games and came off the bench in another five. And no matter what is at stake, every player just wants to play. We're selfish that way. I have no idea why I hadn't played more. Walter obviously knew, but, to this day, I don't. I was fit and available, and when I was called upon, I don't think I ever did too badly. For example, there was the Coca-Cola Cup final on 24 November against Hearts at Parkhead when we won 4–3 and myself and Gazza teamed up brilliantly in midfield. That was a fantastic day that I'll never forget. But I don't think I got a fair crack of the whip during the nine-in-a-row season.

Whenever I got a prolonged run in the side at Rangers, I did well. I'm sure the stats will back that up. But it just didn't happen in 1995/96. I never really got a chance that year. I was getting one game here, one there, coming on as a sub. That kind of inconsistency isn't great in any season. If I'm being honest, I *hated* the nine-in-a-row season – with the exception of that League Cup final – before the night we won it. So as it came to its climax and the club edged closer to sealing the ninth championship, I wasn't sure if I'd play a part at all. That's what I really hated: not having the chance to get involved and help the team when I knew I could contribute.

We played Motherwell on 5 May and it was billed as the day nine-in-a-row would be won. A home victory and it would be ours. There was an incredible party atmosphere at Ibrox that day. There were banners, flags, hats, balloons, and it was live on Sky. This was it. And I was left out of the squad altogether. I was really gutted, but I hadn't played since losing to Kilmarnock on 22 March. And it's fair to say that my preparation for the Motherwell game wasn't exactly ideal.

The day before, I had been travelling in from my house in Bothwell, where I'd moved to in 1996, to training and I had a new BMW car. I'd only had it a matter of days and was still getting used to driving it. But around the Strathclyde Park area, I lost control and spun off the road into a ditch. No one else was involved, but I got a bit of a fright. There was a wee bit of damage, so I had to wait on someone coming out to tow the car away. I phoned Walter to tell him I'd be late for training because I'd been in a minor car crash. I'm not sure if that went against me or not, but I was in the stands for the game against 'Well.

It turned out to be the biggest anti-climax in Rangers' history.

Owen Coyle scored a double for Motherwell to give them a 2–0 win, ensuring the day was a monumental damp squib for the Rangers fans. They'd have to wait a few more days to try to clinch the title at Tannadice in midweek. And I was probably the only Rangers fan in the world who was pleased when we lost that day, selfishly, because I wasn't in the team. I just found it hard to celebrate when I wasn't involved. Fuck that. How can you feel the sense of achievement when you haven't done your bit?

I always say to Coylie now that it was him who made sure I'm part of Rangers' folklore by scoring those two goals. If he hadn't and Rangers had won the game, I wouldn't have played the part I did. Because after the defeat, Walter had to make a few changes for the United game. Durranty had given away a penalty against Motherwell, which Coylie scored, and was bombed altogether. On the Wednesday night against United he wasn't even stripped, which I thought was a bit harsh on a legend like him. I felt it was a shame that, after the contribution he'd made to nine-in-a-row, he wasn't playing in the final game. But I couldn't complain too much, because Walter had given me the nod from the start. And it couldn't really have gone any better for me.

In the 11th minute of the game, I ran past Andy McLaren as if he wasn't there! No, seriously, Davie Robertson took a quick throw in on the left touchline and I got free down the wing. I then whipped a ball in with my left foot and, to this day, I still say Lauders didn't head it. I think he was just running into the box and the ball hit that big mop of hair. But what a feeling after it hit the back of the net. The Rangers fans, who were all over the stadium, were going wild.

I remember Sieb Dijkstra, the United keeper, had two wonder saves from me that night. Listen, a player knows when they've played well. And I know I played well that night at Tannadice. Everything went perfectly for me. I was fit and fresh. We were in the process of clinching nine-in-a-row but, for me, it felt like the start of a season. I was wishing it was the first game of the campaign.

Why did I do so well that night? It was a mixture of things, probably. I wanted to prove a point to the manager after not playing that many games during the season. And also, I knew what was at stake. In my mind I was saying to myself, 'I'm not going to miss this chance to create a bit of history.' I went out and played my heart out. Even Gazza got subbed before me that night, which was *very* unusual. Gazza would never get subbed even if he was having a fucking disaster – which, to be fair, didn't happen too often. When Walter made subs, you knew who was coming off if things weren't going too well.

People say Walter put his faith in me that night, but I don't agree. Walter knew I could play; he'd trusted me to play in big games before, against Celtic and in the Champions League. I don't think there were many times when, on the pitch, he could say I let him down, and Tannadice that night certainly wasn't one of them. I'd been around the place for three seasons by then, so, with all due respect, and even with so much riding on the result for the club, why would I have been worried about playing Dundee United?

We beat a decent United team that night and beat them well, even though the score was only 1–0. It was an amazing game to play in, a brilliant occasion to be part of, and what an incredible feeling at the end. I don't remember the closing stages being too nervous for us. I know the fans will have felt it and the gaffer and the boys on the bench will have been on edge. But on the pitch, I remember we were looking for more goals. When you had Laudrup and Gascoigne on the pitch, why wouldn't you? I don't think United had many chances to deny us our destiny.

Behind us, we had big Andy Dibble in goals that night. It was only his sixth game for the club after he'd been brought in as emergency cover for the Goalie, who was injured. I called big Andy 'Teflon Hands'. He couldn't catch a cold, but he was a cracking shot-stopper. He only came in for that title run-in, but he'd timed his arrival at Rangers to perfection. And he played brilliantly for us.

Big Dibs was a great guy. There must have been a lot of pressure on him, coming in for one of the best keepers any of us had ever seen, at a crucial point in the season. I'll never forget when he was sent home on his first day at Ibrox because he turned up wearing a *green* suit. Archie Knox told him to fuck off back to the Moathouse Hotel and get changed. Daft bastard.

Dibs had come in for his debut at Celtic Park a few weeks previously, which was a pressure-pot game. In essence, that was the day Celtic knew they couldn't stop us equalling their record of nine titles on the bounce. It was a powder-keg atmosphere and I was on the bench.

It was also the day Hateley made his Rangers comeback after being re-signed on a short-term deal because Walter was short of cover. Big Mark and Durranty combined for the goal and we won 1–0. That killed off Celtic's challenge and we did a huddle on the pitch at the end. Check the pictures: I'm right in amongst it.

That was the game when Fergie famously battled with Paolo Di Canio on the pitch. The wee Italian told Fergie that he was going to break his legs in the tunnel after the game. Now, to this day, I know Fergie would just have squashed him. But, I must admit, I now have great respect for Di Canio because when I was at Leicester a couple of years later he was playing for West Ham, who were staying at the same hotel as me, the Stakis. I was standing at reception getting my key when I clocked Di Canio in the foyer. I thought, 'I'm not going to say anything to him.' But Di Canio came straight over and asked how I was. He knew me right away from playing at Rangers and we chatted for a while. He was a top bloke and I respected him for that. He could have just blanked me. And what a great player he was, Di Canio. He was a crazy bastard as well, but I discovered that day in Leicester that he was a complete gentleman off the pitch. You have to remember that emotions run high on the pitch at times – and that was certainly the case at Parkhead that day.

After the final whistle at Tannadice, it was an emotional time. Big Goughie cried getting the trophy on the pitch, which was understandable after everything he'd been through with the club. We were crammed into the tiny away dressing-room, but the champagne was flowing and there was a lot of relief in there. Everyone was so happy. When we got back to Glasgow, we got to Reds and that's when I saw big Mark and Trevor throwing back the shots at the bar.

When I look back now, it's easier for me to appreciate what nine-in-a-row meant to the likes of Walter, Archie, Davie Dodds, Coisty, Durranty, Goughie and Fergie. I just think now how lucky I was to be part of that great team. It's not an easy thing to do, get nine titles on the trot, and I could see the effect it had had on them.

I regard myself as privileged just to have been part of it. To put that cross in for one of the most important goals in Rangers' history was a great feeling. I wish it could have been Laudrup crossing it and me heading it, right enough, but I can't complain too much. All the pictures from that night are of Lauders flying through the air to head it or of him celebrating. I didn't even get into shot – I should've planned it better!

People go on about how surprising it was that I crossed with my left foot. But that's a bit patronising, to be honest. I was two-footed, unlike a lot of players, so it was no problem for me crossing with my left.

The Goalie was actually in Belfast listening to the Dundee United game on a *radio* that night. It wasn't on TV, but, because he was injured, he couldn't bear to be anywhere nearby. So he fucked off to Belfast on a mad one and listened to it instead. What an excuse that is to have a bevvy! He says that when he heard that it was a Charlie Miller left-foot cross and a Laudrup header, he nearly fell off his chair. He refused to believe it was true. He says he was more shocked by my-left footed contribution than Lauders header – but I've told him that's nonsense!

Once the whole furore of nine-in-a-row had died down, the season finished and a squad of us went on a trip to Toronto for a week. It was brilliant and just what we needed after that particular campaign. Myself, Oz, Del, Jukey, Doddsie, big Dibs, Bomber, Coisty and Durranty, we were all there along with a few mates who'd come along. It was incredible. We were well looked after in Canada by the former World Superstars icon Brian Budd, who sadly isn't with us any more, God rest him.

Toronto was the famous trip when big Dibs got his nine-in-a-row tattoo after we'd been out on the lash. Durranty was winding him up, telling him to get a 1690 one, and daft Dibs was asking me, 'Should I?' I was saying, 'Don't be stupid, you daft c***, you'll get lynched!'

I remember us getting on a bus to leave Canada and Davie Dodds was staying behind with Dibs for an extra few days. I asked one of the boys why Davie was staying and they told me it was because he was leaving the club. I was stunned; I had no idea. He was being replaced by Tommy Moller Nielsen. It just shows you how blind I was to things going on around me. I didn't even know that my first-team coach was leaving and I loved Doddsie to bits. He was a top man.

We had seven days over in Toronto, and as the bus was leaving Dibble was shouting, 'Do ten-in-a-row for big Dibs.' The big chancer had only played about six games to get us the nine!

That trip was phenomenal. The amount of drink we put away was ridiculous. Alan Frew, the lead singer in a band called Glass Tiger, is a massive Rangers fan and he also took us under his wing. We were made to feel welcome at whatever pub we went to! Bomber was the main organiser of the boys. By that I mean, he had a beer waiting for you at 9 a.m. every morning and you had to drink it – even though you hadn't got in until three!

Those were magical days for me. I'll never forget those trips, because I have fantastic memories that no one can ever take away from me. I was really fortunate to play in a team that had great men in it, great characters – guys who I'm still in contact with now. That's what happens with Rangers, and at some other clubs it just isn't like that.

It was every Rangers fan's dream to win nine-in-a-row. Millions of people around the world were praying that they'd see it in their own lifetime. And I'm delighted that a wee boy from Castlemilk got to play a huge part in it. I might not have played in too many games that season, but I had made a stack of appearances in the previous two campaigns. No one can ever deny that I made a significant contribution. Even if I'd have played one game in nine years I could have said that I played a small, minute part. But I played in the game that won us it.

The likes of Alan Morton, Jim Baxter, John Greig and Eric Caldow were all great players for Rangers, far better than me. They won trophies, had success in Europe and are rightly regarded as legends at Ibrox. But none of them can say they played their part in nine-in-a-row. As far as I'm concerned, and I'm biased, that achievement eclipses anything any Rangers team has done before or since – and I include the 1972 Cup-Winners'

MEAN STREETS: I could only have been four or five in this picture, running about in Castlemilk where I grew up. I'm sure this is on Stravanan Road, where I lived with my Gran.

FAMILY TIME: Here I am in my Gran's house, where I spent most of my childhood, with my Ma (on the left), my wee sister Susan and my Uncle Benny (on the right), who was like a father to me.

YOUNG GERS: This can't be long after I first joined Rangers BC, so I'd be about nine years old. The team are flanked by our managers Toadie Reid on the right and Alec Partick on the left – both from Castlemilk. I'm second from the left in the back row.

TEAMMATES: Here's another team picture from my Rangers BC days. I'm front row, far right with my mop of black hair. These were some of the happiest days of my life – and there were a few good players in that young side.

SCHOOL DAYS: This is my Windlaw Primary School picture, when I was about eight years old. Judging by the tracksuit top, I was clearly very sporty even then!

AWAY TO FRANCE: I was sent this picture by someone called Francois, after playing in France for Glasgow Schools in the famous black and white stripes. As you can see, there's not a bad crowd watching us in action.

PROUD AS PUNCH: I've just collected my Rangers Boys Club 'Player of the Year' trophy and a Golden Ball for being 'Player of the Tournament' at an event in Denmark. I was presented them by Rangers legend Bobby Shearer.

PALS ACT: Here I am with my Rangers BC teammate Neil Caldwell, who would later join me on the ground staff at Ibrox. We're around eleven years old at the time, with our Glasgow Schools blazers on.

© MIRRORPIX

DRESSED TO THRILL: This is me in a kilt dancing with my cousin Shelley at my Auntie Josephine's wedding. I lived with Shelley for most of my childhood at my Gran's house. The wedding was the same day as the tragic Hillsborough Disaster, 15 April 1989.

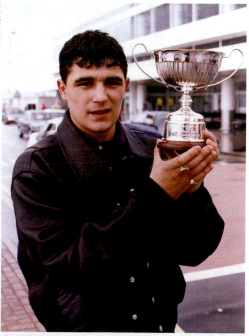

SUPER COOP: I was fortunate enough to spend a day at the races with Davie Cooper shortly before he died, and I realised that he was a proper Rangers legend. I was delighted to pick up the Davie Cooper Skills Trophy, sponsored by the *Sunday Mail*, in 1995.

GOLD FIRM: What a day this was: my first Old Firm game against Celtic at Hampden Park. We won 3–1 and I set up Mark Hateley's goal. Here I am on his back, celebrating the strike – an image that made all the papers the following day.

BREAKING HEARTS: This is me running to the Ibrox crowd in celebration, after I scored the winner against Hearts in a 1–0 victory, back in January 1995. I latched onto a brilliant Brian Laudrup pass and was delighted with the finish.

ON TRIAL: Here I am outside Paisley Sheriff Court, during my trial for assault and breach of the peace after the infamous Fox and Hounds incident. I was found innocent on both charges – this is (left to right) Jimmy 'Five Bellies' Gardner, me, my mate Ricky Ward and one of my fellow accused, Gazza's pal Steven McDermott. Check out the Versace suit that I was caned for wearing by Rangers gaffer Walter Smith.

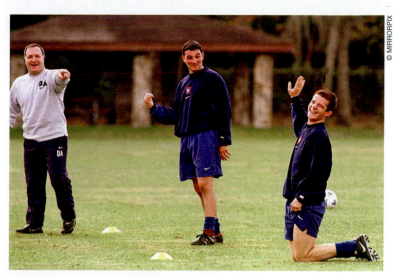

GAME FOR A LAUGH: I didn't see eye-to-eye with coach Dick Advocaat towards the end of my Rangers career, but I liked the Dutchman's methods. This is me sharing a joke with him and Barry Ferguson (right) at training ahead of the 1998/99 campaign.

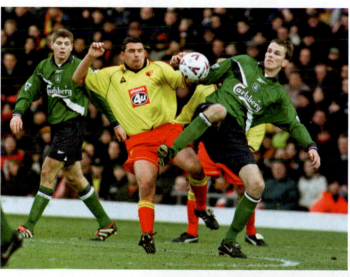

TOUGH AT THE TOP: When I went to Watford, we struggled in the English Premier League against top-class opposition. This is me in a challenge with Liverpool midfielder Dietmar Hamann at Vicarage Road, as England superstar Steven Gerrard looks on.

MISSED CHANCE: This was the year we could and should have won ten-in-a-row at Rangers under Walter, but it wasn't to be. Here, I'm denied a goal by Dundee United's goalkeeper Sieb Dijkstra at Tannadice – but it was one of few chances I got in the side that year.

SINNER TO SAINT:
I had a stinker in the first half of this match against St Johnstone due to a raging hangover, but this goal helped us come back to win 3–2, and played a major part in the club staying in Scotland's stop flight.

IF THE CAP FITS:
I should have had more caps for Scotland, but at least I got one against Poland in 2001. I didn't do myself justice in midfield during a 1–1 draw, but it was great to be in the same squad as my Castlemilk pal, Andy McLaren.

TEAM UNITED:
We had a good team spirit at Dundee United, but on this occasion my aggression boiled over in a match against Motherwell. I'm grappling with Motherwell defender James Okoli, which was quite foolish judging by the size of him.

DERBY DING-DONG: I loved the Dundee derbies against our Tayside rivals, I always seemed to do pretty well in them. They were dogged affairs at times and this is me battling for the ball with Dark Blues stalwart Barry Smith.

GOALS GALORE: At Dundee United, I was given more freedom to get in the box and score. This is me celebrating a strike at Tynecastle against Hearts, joined by my Terrors teammates (right to left) David Winters, Craig Easton, David McCracken and Stuart Duff.

OZ-SOME: The lifestyle and experience of living and playing in Australia was fantastic. We had a terrific group of players at Brisbane Roar when I arrived. This is me with my pals (right to left) Bob Malcolm, Craig Moore and Billy Dodds, who came over to visit.

KIDS PLAY: Here are my two pride and joy. This is a treasured pic of Demi holding her new wee brother Jordan, who is just a baby. I'm so proud of them both.

MODEL GIRL: Demi has grown into a gorgeous young woman. She's destined for great things – if she doesn't follow in her dad's footsteps.

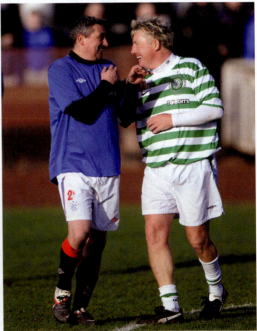

GOLDEN OLDIES: I regularly play in legends games and charity matches for Rangers against Celtic, and it's great to meet up with former players and opponents. Here I am having a laugh with former Hoops idol Frankie McAvennie.

Cup triumph or reaching the UEFA Cup final in 2008. They were both incredible achievements, but with the pressure that was on the team in that nine season, with what was at stake and with the real possibility that there might never be a chance ever again to equal nine-in-a-row, I think the fact that we got over the line and did it is just phenomenal.

It must have been awesome to win the club's only European trophy in Barcelona. The likes of Derek Johnstone, Willie Johnston and Colin Stein will go down in the club's history for that.

But nine-in-a-row – and that night up at Tannadice – is right up there alongside it.

To have been there and done my bit just makes me immensely proud.

7

GAZZA

PAUL GASCOIGNE arrived at Rangers from Lazio for £4.5 million in the summer of 1995.

People often ask me if I was gutted about it in case he took my place in the team, but I can honestly say that wasn't the case at all. Remember, I had won the SPFA Young Player of the Year award the previous season; I was playing well and my confidence was high.

Without being big-headed, I was excited about playing alongside Gazza, this world superstar that I'd watched on TV as a kid playing in Italy. I used to marvel at him on the Channel 4 programme *Football Italia*, which was shown on a Saturday morning. So my first thought when I heard we were buying him wasn't trepidation or fear. I thought it was amazing that we were getting a top-quality player who would add to the squad we already had.

It was a huge signing for Rangers and for Scottish football. But that was what David Murray, the chairman, was all about back then. Right now, it would seem ridiculous to fans to even consider spending that kind of money on any player, never mind someone as good as Gazza. But in those days it was the norm, so it wasn't a huge surprise to the players that he was coming.

That's just what Murray did. He loved a big-name signing that would have Rangers making headlines. He always wanted to kick Celtic by spending more than them and outdoing them when it came to big-money acquisitions. And looking back, getting Gazza for that kind of money was a steal. Murray even managed to get £4 million back when he sold him to Middlesbrough two and a half years later.

My impression of Gazza before he got here was, firstly, what an unbelievable player. But secondly, he appeared to be an absolute nutcase who would be right up for a laugh. I was pretty sure he'd fit right into that Rangers dressing-room we had at the time – and I wasn't wrong.

Paul was an outstanding talent and a world superstar. But from the minute he turned up in Glasgow, that was him. He was just one of the lads. There was no settling-in period for Gazza. From his first day, you'd have thought he'd been at Ibrox for years.

That same year, we also signed big Gordan Petric from Dundee United and the Russian striker Oleg Salenko, who'd scored five goals in one game against Cameroon at the 1994 World Cup.

But Gazza arrived fairly late for pre-season training, and right from the off he was a livewire. I'd heard all the stories about him being unfit, but nothing could have been further from the truth. He was a fit bastard and he could run, all right. He was one of the fittest at the club.

He arrived with this stupid bleached-blond hair and was greeted by thousands of fans outside the front doors of Ibrox. That doesn't happen to every new Rangers signing, but Gazza was special and the punters could sense it.

Everyone knows he's a huge character. But that first day when he walked into the home dressing-room at Ibrox, we were ready for him. No one in there was going to take any shite off him. He must have been in the door two minutes and was being called a 'fat Geordie bastard'. That was the welcome he got. But he loved it; he felt right at home.

That was the good thing about our changing-room at the time. It didn't matter what your background was, where you came from or how much you'd signed for – everyone was treated the same by the players. Big Gordan and Oleg both got a similar kind of reception and – maybe not as much as Gazza – they bought into it too.

I played alongside Paul in his first game for Rangers at Ibrox. It was against the Romanian side Steaua Bucharest in a pre-season friendly tournament that also involved Sampdoria. I quickly realised that the guy was a genius on a football pitch. But that day, he was also a bit naive and got into his first bit of bother in Scottish football.

Ian Ferguson had been winding Gazza up the night before the game, telling him that if he scored on his debut, he had to celebrate in a certain way. Fergie urged him to mimic playing a flute. He assured him that the Rangers fans would love it. Now, anyone from the west of Scotland will know what playing a flute symbolises in Glasgow, but Gazza didn't have a clue. He just wanted to impress the Rangers supporters in his first game at Ibrox. I just couldn't believe he fell for it. But he genuinely didn't know what the fuck he was doing.

We beat Steaua 4–0; Gazza got his dream debut goal and did exactly what Fergie had told him to do. I knew what the reaction would be and, sure enough, there was a huge kick-up in the media about his celebration. He was absolutely caned for it in the press. Celtic fans, and Catholics all over Scotland, weren't too happy about it. Of course, it was a daft thing to do, but I really felt for Gazza on that occasion because he was innocent of nothing other than being a bit gullible.

As a player, Gazza was without doubt the most naturally gifted I ever played with. But he worked on things as well, like his strength. He was as strong as an ox and over the first couple of yards he was razor sharp, even with a ball at his feet. At training, you'd think you had him and then he was away from you in a flash. I must admit, that surprised me about him.

Listen, there were spells in games where he could be a right lazy bastard as well. Often it would be me and Stuart McCall in a midfield trio with Gazza and we knew when there was not a chance of him tracking back. He just wanted the ball.

I always say this about Gazza. He would *loan* you the ball. By that I mean, he'd only give it to you when you had two guys up your arse – because he knew you'd *have* to give him it straight back. He was clever that way. And in his first season at Rangers, he was phenomenal – despite a bit of a ropey start.

Initially, I don't think the Rangers fans were convinced about him, you know. At the start of the 1995/96 campaign, we played the Cypriot side Anorthosis Famagusta in the Champions League qualifier. It was a tie that was worth millions to the club and the type of match in which Gazza would be expected to make a big impact. After all, that was why Murray and Walter Smith had paid the money for him. But Gazza didn't play well in the first leg at Ibrox, which we only won 1–0, thanks to Gordon Durie's late goal. That night, Gazza was nullified by Famagusta's little Bulgarian midfielder Iliyan Kiryakov – who actually earned a move to Aberdeen on the strength of that performance.

The second leg wasn't any easier. Gazza produced a disciplined performance in Cyprus, but it wasn't flashy or flamboyant at all. It wasn't a great start for him.

Even once we'd scraped past Famagusta to reach the Champions League group stages, I remember coming back from our opening match, ironically against Steaua, who beat us 1–0 with that late Prodan goal. The supporters weren't happy at all and, at the airport on landing the punters were giving us all pelters, including Gazza. I think it took him time to realise what it meant to play for Rangers. At first, he didn't appreciate the pressure and level of expectation, because he'd never been at a club like this before. The Italian fans are nuts, but Lazio are nowhere near the size of Rangers.

It's the same for Spurs and Newcastle, Gazza's other former

clubs. They're big in their own right, but they're not institutions like Rangers are. Rangers are one of the most successful clubs in the world. No disrespect to Lazio, Spurs or Newcastle – but how many trophies have they won in their history?

So he wasn't fully aware of what he'd come into at the start, but when the penny dropped, he was frightening at times in that first season for us. He played forty-two games and scored nineteen goals in all competitions for us, which is impressive by anyone's standards. He played a massive part in the club winning eight-in-a-row, and every Rangers fan will remember the day he single-handedly destroyed Aberdeen at Ibrox to clinch the title with a hat-trick.

Unfortunately, I wasn't really giving a fuck that day, because Walter had dropped me from the team after the infamous incident at the Fox and Hounds pub back in March.

But there were so many Gazza highlights that year. Who will ever forget the day he got booked by referee Dougie Smith for giving him a kid-on yellow card? We beat Hibs 7–0 at Ibrox on 30 December and we both got on the score-sheet. The ridiculous booking actually took away from what was a vintage Gazza performance. He scored a stunning solo goal where he beat several Hibs players before slotting past Jim Leighton. But Smith's behaviour when Paul handed him back his card was a disgrace. Talk about a sense-of-humour bypass!

If you watch it again, the reaction of Hibs player Joe Tortolano was brilliant. You can actually see Joe saying to the ref, 'Are you fucking kidding?' – or words to that effect. At that time, it was fashionable to get Gazza in trouble and that was Smith's moment.

Another great memory from that season was the match against Partick Thistle at Firhill in February. We beat them 2–0, thanks to a superb double from Gazza on a really poor pitch. His first was a cracking individual effort from outside the box that flew into the top corner. And for his second, he rounded the keeper after being put through by yours truly.

He would wind up every opponent he was playing against – and he never stopped talking during games. The best example was that day at Thistle. He was in unbelievable form, with both his feet and his mouth, and a good pal of mine, Billy McDonald, was the Jags' victim. Gazza had been virtually unplayable for the full ninety minutes. It was another one of those games where he 'loaned' me the ball quite often. It was a majestic performance and wee Billy couldn't get near him. He took a lot of stick in the aftermath of the game, but Billy was at Rangers with me as a kid and is a great wee guy. He drives a taxi now.

Sadly for him, that day Gazza drove Billy round the bend. He forgot to actually try to play against Gazza and instead he was sucked into what Paul was doing. He tried to rattle him, he was nipping around his ankles all day, but Gazza relished the attention. It just made him play even better.

Eventually, he nutmegged Billy – an absolute cracker – and the wee man was left looking a bit silly. He took a mad fresh-air swipe at Gazza and was sent off. We won the game 2–1 and Paul was just sensational.

By that stage, I was quite close to Gazza. We had become friends off the park, as well as team-mates on it. It's difficult to say how our relationship developed and how we got so close. But he loved playing cards, as I did, and we had a really good card school at Rangers on away trips.

There was one famous game, which I'll never forget, where he done me up like a kipper. We were playing an away game in Edinburgh, against Hibs or Hearts, and we had started a game of three-card brag at the hotel on the night before. I'll try to explain for those not familiar with the game, but it has to start with a '£5 blind' and a '£10 open'. Those were the kind of stakes. But when Gazza was involved that changed. Every time it came to him, he'd say in his daft Geordie accent, '£50 blind.'

So the pot built up and I had a great hand. I had a '1,2,3 stiff', which is an excellent hand. But because he was going '£50 blind',

I had to go '£100 open'. So you can imagine how much cash was involved by now. I reckon there was about £6,000 in the pot and the game was still going. It was down to me or him. Compared with what he was earning and what he was worth, I was small fry, so I was saying to him, 'C'mon, Gazza, fuck sake, open up your hand, because I've got you beat.' And remember, he's 'blind', so he hasn't even seen his hand, but I know I've got a cracker.

The only thing that could beat me was 'three of a kind'. So eventually, he agreed to open up. But, in typical Gazza fashion, he took the first card, *licked* it and stuck it on his forehead so we could see it. It was a 2. I was thinking, 'I've got him.' He then took the second card, did the same, onto the forehead, and it was another 2. Now, I had a 2 in my hand, so there was only one of the fuckers left in the pack. I was thinking, 'There's no way he's got it.' Sure enough, he took the third one, stuck it on his head, and it was the third 2!

I went fucking mental – I couldn't believe it. I was shouting at him, 'You fat bastard!' I was throwing the cards around and going off my head. Let's face it, £6,000 to Gazza was nothing. But to me? That was a hell of a lot of money, and I'd lost. It killed me! He was just laughing his head off. To be fair to him, though, he probably gave me some of it back the next day. That was just what he was like.

On team nights out, he was just incredibly funny. The laughs we had were unreal. One of the best I can remember was with the Tuesday Club. We went along to the District Bar on Paisley Road West, which is Ian Durrant's pub, and Gazza was very smartly dressed with an expensive shirt on. But from the moment we arrived, this little Govan woman was complimenting him on it. She really fancied it and wanted it off his back. For a full hour, she was pestering him for that shirt and – in a nice way – Gazza was telling her to fuck off. But she went on for so long that eventually he agreed to give her the shirt. Obviously, he had to swap with her and she had this grubby Timberland sweatshirt on, so that's what he ended up with.

After a few drinks, someone from the pub offered to drive us to the Steps Bar, which was our favourite haunt on a Tuesday afternoon. But, unfortunately, in the car we began to smell the stench off this jumper Gazza was wearing. It was reeking of body odour. So Gazza just opened the window and threw the jumper – along with a *headrest*, bizarrely – out of the window. Gazza thought it was hilarious that he'd thrown the headrest out as well. You can just imagine him, can't you? After the jumper and the headrest, he was looking for other things to throw out the window. Just like a big kid.

We got to Central Station in Glasgow and there was a Sue Ryder clothes shop right across the street. So Gazza shouted on the driver to stop the car so he could go in and get something to wear because, by this stage, he was bare-chested. Now, bear in mind this was bang in the middle of Glasgow city centre and Paul Gascoigne was running across the road with no top on. But he went into this shop and emerged five minutes later – with a *dress* on. I'll never forget it: a full-length ladies' dress for no apparent reason other than to make us fall about the place with laughter. It was a dark-blue number with white pinstripes. But, as if it was the most normal thing in the world, Gazza just got back in the car and sat down as if nothing had happened. We were in hysterics and it just summed up his mad sense of humour. He spent the rest of the day in the pub with this dress on.

Amazingly, they've still got that very dress downstairs in the Steps Bar.

Now while we were in there, we were about a couple of hundred yards from the Italian Centre in Glasgow, with all the top fashion. Gazza eventually phoned his pal Jimmy 'Five Bellies' Gardner, who was in Newcastle. He told him that he needed new gear right away, jeans and a shirt, so Jimmy got in his car and drove all the way up from England. About five hours later he walked into the boozer with bags from the Italian Centre, with

Gazza's new clothes in them. It was just complete craziness, but that was Gazza's world. Absolute madness.

I remember when his partner Sheryl was pregnant with their son Regan and she wouldn't let Gazza anywhere near her at the time. It was breaking his heart. But she was telling the media he wasn't interested in the baby. It was hurting him – I know that for a fact. He wanted to see her at the hospital, but she wouldn't let him. He responded by joining us on an impromptu trip to London. It was during a break in the season and most of the Rangers boys were on it.

We had a great time down in Soho. I remember all of us, particularly Gazza, giving a down-and-out busker an absolute fortune to play Rangers songs on his guitar. That was brilliant. We were teaching him the tune of 'The Sash' and getting the wee busker to belt it out in the middle of London.

Now, the press weren't aware of that, but we got pelters for going to London in the first place, especially Gazza, because of his family circumstances. But what was so funny was that in one of the newspaper reports it said that Gazza had been on a 'fat guy's back pretending to ride a horse'. Well, I can exclusively reveal that the 'fat man' was in fact Rangers' £2 million centre-half Alan McLaren! That didn't do big Alan any favours, but he and Gazza were great pals. They were like chalk and cheese, but they just got on brilliantly together.

Incidentally, on that same London trip, there was a great story about the Goalie. We were all in a pub, absolutely steaming, and he was up to his usual tricks at the bar, which had a lovely girl serving behind it. We were at the other end of this boozer having a bevvy and a laugh, but the Goalie was in full flow with this barmaid, enjoying a large gin. But as he went to step away from the edge of the bar he got his foot caught in the footrest at the bottom and he fell, crashing his head off the floor. He then tried to get up but, completely drunk, got his foot caught again, and *smash* – his face hit the ground again. He was like someone trying to get out of Jaws' mouth, the way he was sprawling about. There was blood pouring from his face, but we were killing ourselves laughing at him. I remember there was an American couple sitting next to us and the guy said, 'Wow, that's a tough school you lot drink in.'

I loved that line.

Obviously word got back to Walter about what had happened and he had to get the Goalie back up to Glasgow without anyone knowing about it. Unfortunately, it was Bomber who had to drive him up the road, but it could have been Davie Dodds, except he was cleverer than Bomber: when the gaffer asked Doddsie if he had his driving licence with him, he said no, unlike Bomber.

The Goalie woke up the next day and thought he'd been blinded. His face was in some mess and he had no clue as to what had happened to him.

Trips like that were great for the team spirit that Walter was fostering at Ibrox, but we didn't need to get out of Glasgow or the West Coast for a good night out.

I had Gazza in my house loads of times. After the infamous Fox and Hounds incident, he came back to Burnside with me and we were both drunk again. Caroline was raging with me, shouting and bawling. All the while, Gazza just sat on the couch pissed and eating a pizza.

I regularly went out with him and I'd often take some of my pals from Castlemilk along with me. We would go down to Duck Bay Marina, because Gazza stayed at the nearby Cameron House in Loch Lomond. I had stopped smoking the dope by that time, but my mates hadn't and they'd get right into it down there. Obviously, that nutcase would try it as well. He had to get involved because that's just the type of guy he was.

I remember one night in particular. When you roll a joint, a fairly big spliff will be called a 'three-skinner'. But the ones they were rolling that night were 'five-skinners'. They were so big, Jimmy Five Bellies was calling them 'totem poles'. We were upstairs in the snooker room at Cameron House and they were smoking these joints. You could smoke indoors at that time, but because it was dope we had the window open. We were absolutely blootered with the drink, so, for a laugh, Gazza threw the joint out of the window.

Quick as a flash, Jimmy just jumped out after it. He didn't think twice about it. As soon as he was out, Gazza locked him out and shut the window.

Jimmy was stranded on the roof of Cameron House, but he wasn't giving a fuck because, as far as he was concerned, he'd won a watch – he had the doobie all to himself!

Suddenly, Gazza realised that and started shouting him in. But Gazza would have a couple of draws and that would be him stoned. That was what he was like. He was in his bed after a few hours. He'd have a whisky or a gin to finish him off then he'd be snoozing away.

That particular night, me and Jimmy, along with my mates, decided to hit the library in the hotel. As you walk down the corridor, there are rows of wee decorative lights on the wall. But Jimmy, who was well gone by this point, just started punching every one of them off the wall, smashing them to bits. It's scary to think about that now and the fact there would have been other people staying in the hotel. That kind of behaviour is just crazy.

We'd be saying to him, 'Stop that, you fat bastard,' but it was just a laugh to him. When we got to the library, he was ripping up books and throwing them in the big log fire. It was mental. When I think of it now, it was so stupid. But I didn't realise the position I was in. I didn't realise what it meant to play for Rangers at that point.

Anyway, I remember being in that library and the next thing I knew I was waking up in my house. I always took a mate who drove with me and on that occasion it was Brian 'Brains' Adens. I had fallen asleep in the library and stayed sleeping until Brian got me home. But when I'd gone out the night before, I had a brand new pair of Timberland boots on my feet. They were crackers and I was delighted with them. But when I woke up and looked to the floor, there was this horrible pair of worn-out boots lying there.

I said to Caroline, 'Whose fucking shoes are they?'

And she said, 'I don't know, but you were wearing them when you got home.'

It was that bastard Five Bellies, who was about a size 14, who'd swapped boots with me and taken my good Timberlands. His were like a pair of old working boots and I was raging.

That summed me up, though. Contrary to what people think, I'm a rubbish drinker. In some of my mates' company, they'd drink me under the table. I was an amateur compared to them.

Neither could Gazza. I genuinely didn't think he was in danger of becoming an alcoholic back then. To me, he just needed company. That's what he craved. I'd like to think that my mates and I helped him with that loneliness in a very small way.

But listen, it wasn't just me who had mad drinking sessions with him. I know for a fact he'd go round to Coisty's house and they'd get blitzed too. Coisty had a big extension on his house with a pool table and Gazza loved going round there. The bottom line is, the likes of Ally and Durranty were cuter then me about it. Of course they were. I know that now, but I was just a daft boy. They were older and cleverer than me. I was just 'wee Charlie', Jack the Lad.

Gazza was a superstar and I wasn't. Little did I know then, but I had a chance to go on and become a major player like him. I just didn't realise it at the time. And he was never going to tell me to screw the nut and get a grip on myself, was he? I often get asked about our friendship and people wonder whether it was genuine or just superficial. A few folk might think it was just two daft team-mates getting drunk together, but it was more than that. We were mates. I really loved him and I think Gazza loved his pal wee Charlie. I'm sure if you asked Coisty, Durranty or any of the boys in that Rangers dressing-room, they'd say the same thing.

113

I felt for him when he got down and depressed. I could really see it in him when he was playing badly. I could see he was unhappy, but he'd keep it all to himself, because the next day he'd be as high as a kite again, standing in the Ibrox changing-room with his waders on up to his chest and a big fish in his hands. He'd have been out since six that morning.

I could never properly help him with some of his deep-rooted problems. I just tried to help him while he was in Glasgow and make him feel welcome. I could see that his girlfriend, then wife, Sheryl, was never there with him. She was always down in England. He didn't have a lot of family support while he was at Rangers, and I tried, in a tiny way, to provide that for him. I'd like to think it helped him at that time.

When I heard that he'd hit Sheryl, the rumour was that he thought she'd been seeing someone else. She was certainly a lovely-looking woman, but they didn't have the easiest of relationships. My fear was that Sheryl would use Gazza to benefit her own career – but I'm sure she would say differently.

None of the players judged Gazza after the wife-beating incident that was huge news in the Scottish media. He was pilloried for it – some would say quite rightly – by everyone, especially fans of other clubs. I know it's not a nice thing to say now, but when he walked into the dressing-room the day after it was in the papers, we all started singing to him, 'He beats his wife, he beats his wife, he beats his wife – Gascoigne beats his wife.' There's no mercy in a football changing-room. You get slaughtered, no matter how low you might be feeling or how serious a situation is. It wasn't very PC – but that's just the way it was.

Of course, I don't condone Gazza's behaviour. I've got a wife myself and, irrespective of how drunk I am, I can never imagine beating her up. But things happen behind closed doors and a lot went on between Paul and Sheryl. I don't think the guy has a bad bone in his body and that's why I find it hard to accept. Maybe he was a different character at home with her.

114

As a team-mate, however, I had to stand by him. It wasn't easy for Gazza when he moved up to Scotland initally. They bought a house, but it lay empty because he was in Cameron House and Sheryl was in England. When they eventually sold that house, it emerged that Gazza had left a Harley Davidson motorbike in the garage that he didn't even know he had.

If that had been my wife, and I'd have been in his shoes, I'd have told her to get on her bike. Unfortunately, Gazza was smitten with Sheryl. But I don't think there was the same love or affection coming back in his direction. I remember we played Hearts in the 1996/97 League Cup final and we both played really well – I set up one of Gazza's two goals. After we'd beaten Hearts 4–3, I looked up to Caroline in the stand and we both waved to each other. It was a lovely moment. Paul did the same and Sheryl was sitting right next to Caroline, but she didn't even acknowledge him. That's the type of person she was.

That was one of our best days together in a Rangers jersey, that Coca-Cola Cup final at Celtic Park. We went 2–0 up through Coisty, but Hearts fought back to go level through Steve Fulton and John Robertson. That was the famous day when Gazza and Coisty were almost fighting with each other on the pitch. They had a proper go at each other while the game raged on.

Gazza had accused Ally of not reading a pass. He gestured to his head, as if to say Coisty was brainless. But Coisty was having none of it and the row was still going on at half-time. By that stage, Hearts winger Neil McCann was giving us a torrid time.

I was playing at right midfield with big Oz behind me. But we couldn't handle Neilly and we were both booked so couldn't get near him again. Thankfully, Gazza took matters into his own hands and conjured up two wonderful goals for us. The first, a superb solo one, curled past the keeper and the second was from my pass inside the box. I could have turned and shot myself, but he'd have never forgiven me.

We celebrated together after that goal and it was a great feeling.

It was the first cup competition we'd won that I felt I had played a real part in.

Unfortunately, Gazza went through a really tough period after that incident with Sheryl, but, to his credit, he got through it and any dip in form he might have had certainly didn't last long.

When his head was right, Gazza was phenomenal. I find it hard to separate him and Brian Laudrup, because when they were both at their best, my God, no one could live with them. Unfortunately, we rarely saw them at their absolute peak in enough games to make a real difference for Rangers in Europe, but there's no doubt the pair of them had a huge influence on the club winning eight- and nine-in-a-row. They're both legends at Ibrox now, and rightly so.

I was so disappointed when Gazza was sold midway through the 1997/98 season. Walter knows a lot more about football than I do, but I still believe he let him go to Middlesbrough too soon when we were going for ten-in-a-row. He had announced his own plans to quit as gaffer at the end of the season. We also knew by then that Laudrup was going to Chelsea, so it was a turbulent time when all that should have mattered was winning that tenth title.

During the first few months of his time at Boro, Gazza and I kept in touch. A few of the boys and I went down as his guests to Wembley for the 1997 FA Cup final against Chelsea. My pal Lenny Caldwell and I stayed the night in London and had a great time with the likes of Bryan Robson and Gordon McQueen.

I ended up absolutely steaming as usual and I missed my flight up the road the following day. Walter wasn't too happy with that either. I'm sure I made up another lie to him about that – I think this time it was that I was at the maternity hospital with Caroline, who was having Jordan at the time.

I always kept in contact with Jimmy, but with Gazza it was impossible. He changed his mobile number every five minutes – nobody in the world can stay in touch with him. The last time

I spoke to him was in October 2011. After a 1–1 draw with St Mirren he was doing a book launch at Ibrox, but he was in such a state with the drink that he hardly knew who I was. It was such a shame. I didn't feel bad about it, I just felt sorry for Gazza. If it was Coisty who didn't recognise me, I'd be raging and calling him a cheeky bastard, but with Gazza, considering all the demons inside his head, it didn't bother me too much.

I had great times with him and now he probably doesn't even know who I am. But I'm told he barely knows who anyone is – even those who were close to him – which is tragic, because the guy was a genius on the football pitch.

In fact, it wasn't just football. Gazza had never played a game of golf before he came to Scotland and ended up getting his handicap down to about ten. He could play snooker for fun, he was brilliant at tennis – he was good at *every* sport.

Also, he wasn't a silly man. He was intelligent. But he just wanted people to love him. Unfortunately, so many people took advantage of him and I believe that 100 per cent. Gazza couldn't say no to anyone, and that was his biggest problem.

I know he's been in a bad way recently and I deliberately don't look at the YouTube videos of him on the Internet. I also couldn't watch his big interview with Piers Morgan on ITV. I'd heard that Gazza was upset during it and crying – I wouldn't want to see him like that. It would break my heart to see him like that.

I get annoyed at times when I do see him on TV and he's talking about his career but doesn't mention his time at Rangers too much. I genuinely wonder whether it's because he can't remember most of it. But I'm convinced that he had his best spell in club football while at Ibrox.

I fear for him now, I really do. When I read about his problems and his addictions, it is heartbreaking. To see a guy who was such a talent and who has a heart of gold struggling so badly: it's tough to take. It's not about individual addictions to alcohol or drugs with Gazza, it's just addictions full stop. Cars, clothes, chocolate, exercise: you name it, he's been addicted to it at one stage. He's addicted to everything. If it was one thing, he could maybe get help for it. But he's got so many problems, like OCD for instance.

I remember the night before home games for Rangers, he'd come down for dinner at the Hilton Hotel and order fillet steak, every time. But he wouldn't eat it at the table. He'd wrap it up in tin foil and take it upstairs to his room. We'd all go up for a game of cards and he'd sit and eat it in front of us, just like you would a sandwich, or something like that. Then, five minutes after eating it, he'd go into the toilet and bring it back up. He'd be sick nearly every night before games. I was a young kid at the time and didn't know why he did it – I didn't really want to know, I thought it was disgusting. It's only now that I realise Gazza probably had a serious eating disorder. People didn't know that he was suffering from problems like that. He needed help but didn't get it. He was Gazza: happy-go-lucky, joker-in-the-pack Gazza.

I just find it sad that he's ended up the way he is now.

Gazza was a great human being and the most generous person I've ever met. He gave me his Range Rover for a weekend once. Caroline ended up driving it and we loved it.

He also helped me out financially a few times. He always knew when I was struggling, and he couldn't believe that someone like me was only earning around £900 a week basic, while he was getting £20,000 a week. Gazza couldn't understand that and was always willing to help me out. I appreciated that and I'll never forget it.

Possibly, Gazza was a bad influence on me. I accept that and I know some of my old team-mates would probably share that view. But I didn't know it at the time. I just loved his company and so did my mates from Castlemilk. I'd take them all out to have a drink and a laugh with their hero. My Rangers-supporting pals like Rab, Scott Blackett, Ricky Ward and Lenny Caldwell couldn't believe it. They were idolising this guy from the stands at Ibrox every other week. The next thing they knew, they were having a drink with him. Just meeting Gazza was amazing for them.

Do I regret allowing that to happen? Maybe, but I had only been a full-time first-team footballer for about eighteen months by then. I was young and I was probably in awe of Gazza a bit. Remember, early in their Rangers careers the likes of Coisty and Durranty were doing mad things as well, and they went on to become two of the biggest legends the club has ever had. When I came in, I was the only young Scottish boy to come through the ranks.

Craig Moore was the only other product of the youth system involved, but he was Australian and didn't have Glasgow mates to meet up with. Oz could go out for a team night out then go home and spend the next couple of weeks with his missus. After I went out, I had all my mates from Castlemilk wanting to meet for a night out as well, and I didn't want to leave them out.

If I had my time again, I don't think I'd change those times with Gazza. I don't think I wouldn't have gone to Cameron House at least once a month for one of those legendary blowouts. But Walter knew everything. He got wind of everything that was going on, so he'd have known most of what we were up to. Gazza wasn't exactly brilliant at hiding it. If he'd been on a three-day bender, he'd normally start it with a Versace suit on that was worth about £2,000, and, unfortunately, by the third day it would be stinking. This happened twice a month at least, so he'd take Alex Cleland's nice pristine suit, put it on and hang his Versace one on wee Alex's peg at Ibrox. Alex would just shrug his shoulders, take Gazza's suit, go home in his training gear, get the suit dry-cleaned and bring it in for Gazza the next day. That's how laid-back Alex was; he's a great guy.

Everyone loved Gazza at Rangers: the young boys, Peter at the front door, the ladies that cooked our lunches upstairs, everyone. I just wish Rangers had had Murray Park when Gazza and I were around. People might find it hard to believe but there would be days when we'd play head tennis until all hours. If we'd had Murray Park, I'm convinced that a crowd of us, including Gazza, would have been playing five-a-sides or practising free kicks all afternoon. We just couldn't do that at the training grounds Rangers had for us at that time. We all had to be on a bus back to the stadium at a certain time.

Gazza's talent let him get away with murder. But Walter forgave him for what he did on the park on a Saturday, which is fair enough.

Sadly, I wasn't afforded that luxury.

8

IBROX EXIT

RANGERS played a huge part in my life for the best part of thir-teen years. From the moment I first put on my blazer for Rangers Boys' Club at the age of ten to crossing for Brian Laudrup to head home the goal that clinched nine-in-a-row. I became immersed in the club. I'd had trials and tribulations at Ibrox, ecstatic highs and devastating lows. I'd been through it all with Rangers, but it only made the strength of feeling I had for the club even stronger.

Maybe when I was younger, I took being a Rangers player for granted, but in later life, I learnt to appreciate it a lot more. And that's why, even now, it makes me angry talking about how I left Ibrox in 1999.

Walter had announced that he was leaving midway through the season with the team trying to win a record tenth title. That was a decision I think backfired. I've already said that selling Gazza during that campaign was a big mistake, as was trying to introduce too many new signings in one season. But what do I know? Anyway, we failed to win ten-in-row, as Wim Jansen steered Celtic to the championship in his first year at Parkhead. The fans were gutted. They had rejoiced at winning the ninth title, but they craved number ten to get one over on their Old Firm rivals.

When Walter left, I had no idea what the future would hold

for me as a Rangers player. He was all I really had known as a manager up until that summer of 1998. Towards the end of the season, we'd heard that it would be Dick Advocaat taking over, and my first reaction was excitement.

As much as I'll always be grateful to Walter for the chance he gave me at Rangers – something I'll never forget – I often felt a bit harshly treated during my time under him, for reasons I've set out already. As I've said previously, I was a soft target and someone who was easy to pick on, so I was intrigued as to what Advocaat would be like. He had an outstanding pedigree in Holland with PSV, as well as with the Dutch national side. He might have been nicknamed 'the Little General' and was someone who was renowned for being a strict disciplinarian, but that didn't worry me. I was willing to knuckle down for Advocaat and fight for a starting place in his Rangers side. I thought it could be a bit of a fresh start for me at Rangers. I thought that he might fancy me from the off and put a bit more faith in me than Walter had shown. But unfortunately it didn't work out the way I had planned, and this is the first time I've spoken about how my association with the club came to an end.

I can tell you that I felt really let down when I realised my time was up at Rangers. It was one of the major low points of my career. Let me put the record straight first by saying that I actually quite liked Advocaat. I had a lot of time for him and I really enjoyed his coaching, but in the end I felt let down by him. Dick said I'd keep my place in the team if I played well, but he failed to stick to his words. I felt I could have been playing out of my skin during his first season and I still wouldn't have merited a regular start as far as he was concerned. I suppose it was his opinion against mine about whether or not I was playing well enough to earn a place in the team. I think I had done enough to deserve a chance, but he was the boss.

If you look back at the archives, my last ever start for Rangers was against Dundee in a league game on Wednesday, 27 January

1999, at Dens Park. I scored two goals and we won 4–0. I was awarded the 'Man of the Match' award and a bottle of champagne. It was a game I felt I played really well in and the fans gave me a terrific reception that night. But incredibly, in true Advocaat style, I was back on the bench again on the Saturday. I think I got on for one minute against Aberdeen at Pittodrie in the game that followed the Dundee victory. And to be honest, that was when I knew everything was coming to an end – because there is only so much you can take as a player.

Remember, I'd played for Rangers from a very young age. I felt that by that time I deserved to be treated a little better. I was desperate to play games for the club, but Dick thought nothing of messing me about like that. He never understood how I felt and I suppose that was at the heart of the problem.

Dick arrived in the summer of 1998 and I had one year left on my contract. But he obviously liked what he saw, because I signed a two-year extension, which I was absolutely delighted about. When he first came in, he told me that my fitness wasn't good enough to be in the squad. That was fine. I wasn't too happy, but I accepted it. He was the new manager and I had to do what he asked. That's why I wasn't involved in his first game, a UEFA Cup qualifier against the Irish side Shelbourne at Prenton Park in Tranmere.

Dick had a bit of a nightmare in the first forty-five minutes in the job. Shelbourne were 3–0 up at the break in the first leg before he made a few substitutions that changed the game in our favour. We scored five goals in the last half-hour to win 5–3.

I was training with the kids initially, because Dick didn't feel my fitness was good enough for the first team, but I was determined to prove myself to him. I liked his training methods, which were very different to Walter's. He'd opened my eyes up a bit. On pre-season with Walter and Archie, it was just run, run, run, as fast as you can. But with Dick, it was more thought out. I experienced similar coaching techniques in Norway and Belgium later in my career. Dick wouldn't ask me to run as fast as a guy who was naturally fitter than me. It makes no sense. Why would he? In the same way, he wouldn't ask someone who was less talented than me to do something on the pitch he wasn't technically capable of.

He brought in some brilliant players in his first season. The likes of Giovanni van Bronckhorst arrived from Feyenoord, Arthur Numan from PSV and Andrei Kanchelskis from Fiorentina – and they were all big-money buys. But, arguably, the biggest surprise to me was Rod Wallace, who was signed on a free from Leeds United. What a player he was, and he was a lovely wee guy off the pitch as well. I loved Rod.

Gio was an outstanding talent. He was quite arrogant, the way Dutch players normally are, but I actually liked that about him, and it was no surprise to me that he went on to achieve loads of success in his career with Barcelona and Holland.

I wasn't sure how Dick would take to me at first. I had no idea if he even knew who I was before he agreed to become Rangers' gaffer. It did surprise me when he decided to build the team around Barry Ferguson, having never seen him play either. That was brilliant for Barry, and I was really pleased for him because he was my mate, but it hurt me a bit because clearly he saw Barry as his playmaker in the middle of the park – a role I felt I could have filled.

I told Dick that I'd be happy to sign the new contract as long as he gave me a chance to play, an opportunity to prove myself. But I was regularly on the bench for him at the start of that 1998/99 season. I was quickly running out of patience at my lack of game time. I waited right up until January and a home Scottish Cup tie against Stenhousemuir. I was basically saying to him, 'C'mon to fuck, if you don't give me a chance in this game, I'll never get one.' I was a sub almost every week, getting on for two minutes here and five minutes there. However, I have to say I was earning good money.

At that time I was on £5,000 a week and £2,000 for every

124

appearance I made. Then you had a £1,200 win bonus, so sometimes I'd be getting £10,000 a week for five minutes of football on a Saturday. It was some difference to what I'd been on under Walter! But that wasn't the point. I wanted to start games. I really wanted to play for Dick.

If I'd wanted to, I could have just sat there for another two years, picked up my money and hardly kicked a ball. I could have been greedy, but I wanted to play. I know some people might not think it, but I've always had morals in life. When I was a kid, I desperately wanted to be a footballer, so I've always wanted to play, as opposed to sitting on my arse every weekend.

Finally, he started me against Stenhousemuir. It was a no-brainer for him. But, needless to say, I didn't play too well. It was tough, because I hadn't started a game all season up to that point, and I was on a hiding to nothing against Stenny, because if you win 8–0, it's expected because of the quality of player we had against lower-league opposition. But if you win 2–0, as we did that day, everyone complains that it wasn't good enough. It was a horrible game, to be honest, and I knew I hadn't done myself justice.

Incredibly, Dick kept me in the side for that midweek game at Dens, and on that occasion I was close to my best again. I went home with the champagne and thought I might just have played myself into his team now. I felt I could become a regular and really start taking off.

But after the long journey up on the Saturday to Aberdeen, I got on for a single minute in a 4–2 victory. I was stunned and felt really low. At that point, my attitude was 'fuck this'. I was ready for leaving there and then, but Dick didn't want to let me go and I was *always* in his squad. Yet I was getting more and more fed up and eventually, in March, he agreed to let me join Leicester City on loan.

It was real last-minute stuff. I remember having to dash over to Ibrox to sign my release forms so the deal could be pushed through. Looking back now, I wish I hadn't done it. I rushed into it and it was a spur-of-the-moment decision. I had my angry head on because I wasn't playing as often as I'd have liked. But, thinking back now, if I'd have stayed I would still have been part of a brilliant treble-winning side in Dick's first season. His team won the title at Parkhead in sensational style with a 3–0 win. We had beaten St Johnstone in the League Cup final earlier in the campaign and went on to beat Celtic in the Scottish Cup final, thanks to a goal from wee Rod. I gave all of that up to go out on loan, and I wish I hadn't bothered.

I wanted to play football, but what I didn't realise back then was that if you leave Rangers – or a similar-sized club like Celtic, Manchester United, Liverpool or Arsenal – you only go down the way after that. As a footballer, you don't think like that, but as soon as I wasn't at Rangers, it hit me. You suddenly realise how big a club it is.

I joined Leicester until the end of the season but got injured in my first start for them against Newcastle. It was a challenge from Gary Speed, God rest him, but it put me out for a few months. That was me back up the road to Ibrox already for treatment.

I only made three sub appearances for the Foxes and that one start at home to Newcastle on 8 May 1999. It was a good club and I played with some cracking players, like Neil Lennon, Robbie Savage, Muzzy Izzet and Emile Heskey. I don't have a bad word to say about Martin O'Neill either, who had signed me. It just wasn't to be for me at Filbert Street.

By the end of the campaign at Ibrox, I had started just two league games under Dick, one of which was my Dundee 'Man of the Match' performance and the other a 1–1 draw up at Aberdeen back in September.

I knew my future with Advocaat at Rangers was uncertain at best, but my gut feeling, after the experience at Leicester, was to stay and try to fight for my place. Sadly, that outlook was to change dramatically with one clatter of my letterbox during that summer.

Despite having a year left on my contract, I received a letter through my door from the chairman, David Murray. It told me that I was to report for pre-season training with the *reserve* squad in the *away* changing-room on the squad's return date. I was flabbergasted. I just couldn't believe it. My good mate Derek McInnes got the exact same letter – and amazingly he'd started in the Scottish Cup final win against Celtic just a few weeks before. He'd played in the last game of the season for Dick to seal a treble.

In fact, it's frustrating when I look back because I think that I might have played instead of Derek in the cup final at Hampden if I hadn't joined Leicester. Del was brought in from nowhere by Dick into the side that day. He hadn't even been involved in squads before then so I could well have been given the nod.

Anyway, we couldn't understand why we'd been treated so badly by the club. I was disgusted and embarrassed. I was also raging with Murray, who I'm convinced had something against me. I thought that David didn't like me, and I didn't like him. I still don't to this day. Yes, he did a lot for the club, but Rangers means everything to me and I was never sure if it really meant the same to him.

I took the blow on the chin. I didn't call Murray or Advocaat. I just turned up for training with the kids when I was supposed to. Derek had actually taken the news even worse than me. He shouldn't have, because I had been at the club far longer than him, but it was because he'd played in the cup final and had then been ditched so soon after. That must have hurt a lot and I felt for Del, who was – and still is – one of my best friends. It was completely wrong of Rangers to treat him in that way: he'd just helped win them a major trophy against their Old Firm rivals and he was a supporter of the club, who'd fought hard to earn the right to play for them.

If Dick had come up to me or Del and said, 'Look, you're not going to be part of my plans, I'd like you to move on,' we could probably have accepted it a lot easier. But having spent the past four years in the home dressing-room at Ibrox, to get dumped into the away one was a real kick in the guts for me. The last time I'd been in there was as a YTS apprentice, cleaning it as part of my chores.

Despite all of this, on my first day back Dick walked past me in one of the stadium's corridors and said, 'Aw, Charlie, how are you?'

I said, 'You can fuck off.' I told him I didn't want to speak to him.

Dick wasn't happy and he called my agent, John Viola, to complain. He told John that he'd 'lost his respect for me'. But was the letter sent to Derek and me not disrespectful? I had lost my respect for him by then and I knew I was finished with Dick after that. I don't think he understood the significance of that letter. He didn't know what the club meant to guys like Del and me. This was the club we'd grown up supporting and had gone on to win nine-in-a-row with.

The club was part of us and vice versa, but Dick didn't get it. He was ruthless, and maybe that's the way you have to be as a manager at the top level. But I still think he could have done things differently. We just wanted to be dealt with face to face. Instead, the club decided to treat two of their own, two Glasgow boys, like shite.

And I believe that's always been the case at Rangers. It's strange, isn't it? They'll fall over themselves trying to help foreigners or English players at Ibrox. But I think they could treat the local lads who achieved a lot at the club so much better.

Just two years ago, the club invited me back to be part of their 140-year anniversary. They called me to say they'd book me into a hotel for the night, which I was grateful for. But when I asked if I could get a couple of spare tickets for my family to attend the game, they said they couldn't help me. It's ridiculous the way they treat the Scottish lads at times. The likes of Nacho Novo, Lorenzo Amoruso and Michael Mols are rightly regarded as legends at Ibrox. They were terrific players and I love them all. But why should they be treated any better than the likes of myself, or Derek, or Alan McLaren, or Alex Cleland, who were all part of the club's nine-in-a-row success? With all due respect, the likes of Mols or Amoruso had no emotional attachment to Rangers before they arrived, and they were only around for a few seasons. I'm not jealous of their iconic status at the club. I'm just disappointed that the club don't try to look after the Scottish boys more.

Anyway, I was dumped in the reserves and training with John Brown's young boys at Murray Park. I just didn't want to be there and, in retrospect, I didn't do Bomber any favours. I had played with Bomber at Rangers and we got on really well. He's a proper club legend, a Hall of Fame member, who would have run through a brick wall for his team-mates. But it's fair to say that we had our wee fall-outs. He had become a coach while Walter was still in charge and there was a spell where we didn't see eye to eye.

I've heard that Bomber still tells people I was the best young player he's ever seen at Rangers. If that's true, it's a lovely compliment, and I'll always have time for Bomber. However, we'd had a real barney before Dick had even arrived at Rangers when, again, I'd been told to train with the youths. I can't even remember what I had done this time to annoy Walter, but I felt Bomber had changed when he'd become part of the backroom staff at Ibrox and I found it hard to deal with. I know now that he was only trying to better me and help me, but I just couldn't see it at the time. In the mornings I had to take my daughter to school, so I was looking for a bit of leeway in terms of the time I was arriving at training. The young boys all have to be in for 8 a.m. but I told him I'd be struggling to make that because of Demi. I told him I could be in for just after nine, but he was having none of it. I said to him, 'C'mon, Bomber, cut me a bit of slack,' but his attitude was, 'Just get on with it, Charlie.'

Then one day I was waiting behind to do a weights session that normally started around 1 p.m. It usually only lasted about half an hour. But Bomber came in and said I had to wait until 4 p.m. to do it – because he had to go and pick *his* daughter up from school!

I said, 'Are you taking the piss?'

He just shrugged and said, 'You're staying,' and I said, 'Am I fuck.' Suddenly, in the corridor at Ibrox outside the home changing-room, we came to blows. It was Bomber who swung for me first, by the way! I never thought he'd ever try to hit me, but he did and there was a bit of fisticuffs.

Jörg Albertz had to come and split the two of us up. Bomber then went into the manager's office and I retreated to the dressing-room. Walter soon came to see me and said, 'Here, you, who the fuck do you think you are?' I didn't tell the gaffer that Bomber had gone for me first. He saw it as me trying to pick a fight with one of his coaching staff.

Back then, I lost a bit of respect for Bomber after the incident. We'd played in the same team together and I don't think you should ever swing for one of your own team-mates. To be fair to him, he forgot about it quickly and we started to get on again. It was done and dusted. And now? I think the sun shines out of his arse, because he's helped me a lot and is a top bloke. We still go for a drink together, and until last year I used to see him in Hong Kong every year for the Soccer Sevens tournament that I normally play in.

By the time I was actually working under Bomber, after Dick had demoted me, my head was gone. And I let Bomber down badly. In fact, I let myself down, because I wasn't giving a fuck. I should have been a great example to the young kids coming through at Ibrox, but I wasn't. If it was now, the way I am today, I'd have knuckled down and done what I had to do. But back then I didn't. Derek did, to be fair to him; he was brilliant for the young boys, even though he'd felt badly let down by the club as well. At that time, I just hated being there. I hated being treated the way we were.

Listen, I never wanted to leave Rangers. But at that point I felt as if I *had* to. Going to Leicester and then Watford were just opportunities to play football.

The annoying thing is, I could have signed a pre-contract with Watford in January 2000 and made myself a few quid. Instead, I agreed to join them three months earlier in the September and got Rangers £450,000 for me. How fucking stupid was that? I think John Viola asked Murray for a £100,000 pay-off and he told him, 'No, he's getting fuck all.' So I got nothing when I left Rangers and moved to the English Premiership for *less* money than I was on at Ibrox. I must be the only guy in history who's moved from Scotland to England's top flight and been worse off financially.

As I've already said, in my opinion Graham Taylor proved to be one of the worst managers I ever worked under. He just didn't want to play football in the right manner. Looking back, I could have signed for Charlton Athletic at the same time, but I had given Taylor my word and didn't want to go back on it. Hindsight's a wonderful thing.

One positive thing about my time there is that I ended up forging some great friendships with people like Neil Cox, Richard Johnson, Allan Smart, Robert Page and Nordin Wooter. There's no doubt I could have played at the top level in England. I'm pretty sure if you asked any of the players I played with or coaches I worked under, they'd say the same thing. My big regret is that I moved to the wrong club.

I remember turning up on my first day at Vicarage Road and being handed a giant Le Coq Sportif bag, which was almost as big as me. I thought, 'What the fuck is this for?' I was told that it was my kit bag and I had to take my training gear home every day to wash it. This was the Premiership in England! I couldn't believe it, but, sure enough, we had to wash our own kit every day. So you can imagine how mine smelt some days at training! I thought I had completed a two-year apprenticeship at Rangers to ensure

I'd never need to wash kit ever again. But that summed up my experience at Watford as a whole.

Taylor had over-achieved by getting that squad of players into the Premiership in the first place. It wasn't the right club for me. I was a playmaker. I was keen to play the ball on the deck, in the right way. But that's not what he wanted. He wanted me to tackle and win balls in the air, which just isn't my game at all.

Don't get me wrong, I got the chance to play against some top players while I was down there. I went toe to toe with Steven Gerrard when we played Liverpool. I also believe the Premiership then had even better players than it does now. Think about it: Manchester United had just won the treble in 1999, so I got to pit my wits against the likes of David Beckham, Roy Keane and Paul Scholes, as well as against Gianfranco Zola at Chelsea and David Ginola at Spurs, among others.

Talking of Beckham, I have to mention the time he scored one of the greatest goals of all time for United, with a pair of *my* boots on. On 17 August 1996, Becks announced himself on football's world stage with a goal against Wimbledon at Selhurst Park, which must have been shown a million times since. He scored a cracker from the half-way line into poor keeper Neil Sullivan's net, and the goal is repeated every time there's a Beckham compilation on TV or the best moments ever from the Premiership. But not a lot of people know that I played my part in it and helped him on the road to superstardom.

At the time, I had broken into the Rangers first team under Walter and was rated as one of the up-and-coming young players in British football. I had earned a boot deal with Adidas, who Beckham was also signed up with. But on that day, he needed a pair of boots urgently. I don't know if his had burst or if he'd lost them – it could have been anything – but shortly before the Wimbledon game, he needed a pair of Predators ASAP.

When he contacted Adidas, they had to get him a pair as quickly as possible and just happened to have a pair of mine, which had been custom-made and were waiting to be delivered to Glasgow. They even had my name, Charlie, embroidered on the tongue. But because Becks happened to the same size as me, they decided just to send him mine. So there you go. David Beckham scored one of the most iconic goals of all time with a pair of Charlie Miller's boots on. I'm pretty sure he's kept them and they're on display at his football academy in England.

Needless to say, when I eventually did receive my boots with 'Charlie' on the tongue, I didn't score from the halfway line with them!

Anyway, Caroline had moved down to Watford with the kids. We bought a house on the outskirts, and at first we were determined to make a go of it. I went down there with my eyes wide open and genuinely thought, 'I'm going to do well here.' It should have been the start of a new life for us all, but it just didn't work, on or off the pitch. I wasn't getting a regular game and gradually became unhappy. I was drinking and gambling too much, which was making matters worse.

Caroline could see me going off the rails a bit first-hand and – although I had no idea at the time – she actually phoned Taylor herself at one point to ask why he wasn't playing me! It's certainly not the done thing for your wife to call the manager and question his team selection. When Taylor told me, I said, 'Don't be daft, what are you talking about?' But it was true: she'd phoned him. I felt it made me look really weak and I had a go at Caroline for it. To be fair to her, she was probably a bit homesick and she could see how things were affecting me. She was only trying to help, but she probably went the wrong way about it.

In the summer of 1999, after Watford had been relegated, I knew I had to get out. I played one game for the club the following season, a 0–0 League Cup draw against Cheltenham in August, when I came on as a sub for fifteen minutes. It was clear that Taylor wasn't going to play me in the Championship and he could probably see that I was desperate to leave. JV, as I called

John Viola, had told me Dundee United were interested, and they made their move in November. But the night before I was due to sign, I got absolutely paralytic drunk at home in Watford.

I had fallen asleep on the floor when Caroline got a call to say I had to be up in Dundee the following morning. It was perfect timing, as usual. Thankfully, I don't suffer too badly with hangovers and I managed to make the early flight from Heathrow. How I got from Glasgow to Dundee, I can't actually remember. I was still a bit worse for wear, to say the least.

I hardly even negotiated with Dundee United; I just signed the deal because I was so keen to get out of Watford. But, again, I cost myself money. I agreed to a £100,000 pay-off from Watford even though I had two years left on a contract that was worth £4,500 a week, with £1,500 appearance money. However, it was a chance to get back to Scotland and I felt as if I could flourish under the manager, Alex Smith. Caroline was happy too, because she could get back closer to her family.

That day I signed, I remember Craig Easton picking me up from a hotel in Dundee. I didn't really know Easty at that point and he turned up in a silver Beetle. It wasn't exactly what I was expecting and I immediately gave him pelters for driving a girl's car. I trained that morning at Camperdown, next to the ice rink in Dundee. The facilities were terrible; it was like being back on a bit of grass in Castlemilk. But I didn't care: I was back in Scotland. I signed my contract after training, and I was ready to produce some of the best football of my career on Tayside.

9

UNITED FRONT

TO say I had a challenge on my hands going to Dundee United would be an understatement. I arrived at the start of November 2000 and we were rock bottom of the Scottish Premier League. Incredibly, we'd taken just *two* points from our opening thirteen games before I got there, and we were already eight points behind St Mirren, who were the team closest to us in the table.

Alex Smith, the manager, was under pressure. When I got to United, without being disrespectful, the squad lacked any real quality. Almost immediately, I felt I was the best player we had. But that was probably good for me, because it gave me a bit of responsibility. I felt I had to try to get us out of the rut we were in.

Alex had put a lot of faith in me and I wanted to repay him. He might have been struggling a bit with United at the time, but he was a top coach. And he let me play. He was the only gaffer in my professional career who consistently played me in my favoured position, just behind a front two. That's where I could create chances, penetrate teams and do damage.

I loved Alex. Remember, aside from Sir Alex Ferguson, he was arguably the greatest manager in Aberdeen's history. Yet they got rid of him when he lost the league title to Rangers on the final day of the 1991/92 season. Thinking back now, how crazy is that?

Anyway, my arrival in 2000 didn't exactly yield immediate

success. I lost my first three games, including a derby against Dundee. Finally, on 25 November, we picked up a 3–2 victory over Dunfermline and I scored the winner with a late penalty. Even then, it was 2 January before we got another win, this time against Motherwell.

We were in the bottom two for the whole campaign but just managed to edge out St Mirren, who were relegated with just one game left. It was a poor campaign for a club of United's size, but I felt as if I'd made a big contribution to us staying up. I'd played twenty-nine games and scored six goals. The highlights were beating Dundee 3–2 at Dens Park in January 2001, and knocking Rangers out of the Scottish Cup, thanks to David Hannah's goal.

I played well towards the end of the season and we actually won our last four matches, which were vital to our survival. The crucial one, away to St Johnstone, still brings a smile to my face now. The boys who weren't in the squad, or were unavailable for selection, decided to have a few beers on the Friday night, before the trip to McDiarmid Park. I knew I'd be playing, but, stupidly, I decided to join them in having a bevvy. I ended up absolutely wasted, with a horrendous hangover on the morning of the game.

At half-time we were 2–0 down, and I hadn't kicked my arse and had already missed a penalty. I felt terrible. At the break, I could tell Alex knew I wasn't right, but this was a game we desperately had to win if we wanted to stay up. I remember Alex pleading with me, saying, 'Charlie, for fuck sake, just give us something!'

I don't know how I managed it, but I somehow got myself together for the second half. Saints had Paul Hartley sent off and that gave us the lift we needed. I got us back into it with a great diving header, and we got another two in the last nine minutes through Easton and Derek Lilley to secure a priceless three points. That day was pivotal to us staying in the top flight and I felt I had achieved what I'd set out to do when I signed. Alex's squad might have been short on ability, but we had a terrific spirit in that dressing-room.

That season, I also won my first – and last – full Scotland cap. But I'll get on to that later.

The following campaign, Alex got us up to eighth position in the league, but it still wasn't great. I had scored our first goal of the season, in the derby against Dundee, but we had to salvage a 2–2 draw, thanks to Jim Hamilton's last-minute equaliser. And it was a fairly disappointing period after that. Hibs knocked us out of the League Cup – not helped by a red card for yours truly – and our Scottish Cup hopes were ended by lower-league opposition in the shape of Ayr United.

By the end of it, Alex's position was still under scrutiny. A club of United's stature should always be in the top half of the Scottish Premier League – that should be the minimum requirement.

By the start of the 2002/03 season, there was speculation that United were being bought over by millionaire businessman – and United fan – Eddie Thompson. Alex had to impress the prospective new owner, but we let both him and ourselves down. We won just one of our opening nine games – a 2–1 victory over Aberdeen. And just two games into Thompson's reign at Tannadice, Alex was sacked following a 2–1 defeat to Hibs. I felt terrible for him, but I also felt I had given my all for Alex and when a new owner comes in, it's inevitable that they'll want to bring in their own man.

Thompson's man was Ian McCall, who was doing a great job at Falkirk. But initially Thompson couldn't get him, and United legend Paul Hegarty was put in charge until the end of the season.

Heggy is a great human being and I felt he was shafted by United. He didn't even get to the end of that campaign, because Thompson finally agreed a deal with McCall. Paul was treated poorly, in my opinion, by a club he'd served so well. He, along with Maurice Malpas, had the respect of all the boys, but, lacking quality, we struggled to get results. I'd like to think, during that

137

tough spell, Heggy and Mo respected the effort I was putting in on and off the park for the club.

During that time I had a bad experience myself. It was another day at Ibrox I'll never forget, but, sadly, it was for all the wrong reasons this time. It was 14 December 2002 and we were scudded 3–0 by Rangers. Barry Ferguson scored a hat-trick. When I had gone back to Ibrox before as a United player, I had received a pretty poor reception from the Rangers fans, which was disappointing. But on this occasion, it was even worse, and I had done nothing wrong.

Dutch player Fernando Ricksen did me with a tackle to my knee and got a straight red card for it. Jamie McCunnie had taken a throw-in, and as I played the ball, Ricksen came through the back of me. It was a knee-high challenge and the referee had no hesitation in sending him off. There was no doubt about it – it was a red card.

If my leg had been planted on the ground, he'd probably have broken it. But instead of the Rangers fans having a go at Ricksen for leaving them with ten men, I got roundly booed by the supporters, and it hit me hard. After the time I'd spent at the club and everything I'd achieved, I felt I deserved better. I remember after the game, I was crying in the Cooper Suite at Ibrox. Big Alex McLeish was the Rangers manager then and he saw me upset in the corridor. He came over and consoled me and told me to keep my head up.

Alec Patrick, my old manager at Rangers BC, is mad about the club, a real Bluenose. He's a season-ticket holder and was there that day, and he told me when people were jeering me from the stands, he was trying to stick up for me with the punters. When they were giving me stick, he'd stand up and shout back at them.

Ricksen did a lot of stupid things during his time at Rangers and this was one of them. He'd tried to injure an ex-Rangers player who'd been part of nine-in-a-row and got himself sent off, but the fans were having a pop at me. That left a real sour taste in my mouth. I was gutted.

I know Fernando is really ill right now and it's tragic that he's suffering from motor neurone disease, but I thought it was harsh on me at the time. Listen, the fans were only supporting their own player, I understand that, but I hadn't done anything wrong. I was part of one of the greatest teams in the club's history and when I played I was probably on twenty times less money than Fernando earned at Ibrox!

I've actually been to a few functions with him recently and we're good mates now. I joke with him that he managed to turn the entire Rangers support against me with one tackle. He's a good guy and I really admire the way he'd battling his illness. I'm full of admiration for him now.

Thanks to Barry, we were losing 3–0 to Rangers and by that stage the supporters were getting to me, booing every touch I had. I remember saying to myself, 'Fuck this,' and I was desperate to score against them. So late in the game, I managed to beat three or four players and hit a cracking shot. I reckon it would have been one of the great Ibrox goals, but Stefan Klos pulled off a brilliant save.

After the game, my United team-mate Allan Smart said to me, 'Charlie, I wish they'd been booing you from the first minute!'

That's a big reason why I don't go to Ibrox regularly to support Rangers now. I'd never say that I gave any less than 100 per cent against Rangers when I played at United, but after that game, I was trying extra hard, giving 110 per cent to do well. Sometimes the fans forget easily. I took a couple of spankings against Rangers – and Celtic – while I was at United. But we beat my old club on a few occasions and I enjoyed every one of those games. I suppose that's football, and maybe I should look at it differently – maybe they were booing me to put me off my game, because they knew I was capable of doing them some damage.

Anyway, Ian McCall was officially appointed as our new boss in January 2003 and brought with him Gordon Chisholm and Tony Docherty as his backroom team. I'll say one thing for McCall – he had a bit of attitude. He was bold and brash, and fancied himself as a proper gaffer.

I will never forget his first day as Dundee United boss. He said to the boys, 'Right, the ones who are going to be on the pitch, put your boots on. And the ones who are going to be trackside, put your trainers on.'

I was our best player by a mile, so I put my boots on right away and he said, 'Fuck, you're confident eh?'

Right away, I thought, 'This guy has a bit of a hit for himself.'

In his first week, he dropped our regular goalkeeper Paul Gallacher and put Alan Combe in. McCall's words were: 'Things have to change here.'

That was fair enough. We hadn't been doing well enough as a team or a club, and he wanted to make an impression with big decisions. I can understand that. But poor Comber was sent off after just twelve minutes of McCall's first game in charge against Motherwell on 1 February 2003. Then Gal came on and did well. We won 2–1 with ten men and I got the winner, so it was a great start for me.

At first, I did well for McCall at Tannadice. I was happy and enjoying my football. Off the pitch, we lived in Broughty Ferry and loved it. It was a beautiful place to stay. Caroline and I met loads of nice people, like Gal, and he and his wife Belinda became close friends. Big Stevie Thompson and his missus, Joanne, were the same.

McCall came in and – with Eddie Thompson's backing – was allowed to make changes right away. McCall's remit was clearly to have us challenging in the top six the following year. He brought in my mate Derek McInnes, which I was 100 per cent delighted about. He also signed Tony Bullock, Scott Paterson, Alan Archibald and Barry Robson, who had been my boot boy at Rangers. He'd even stayed with me and my uncle Benny when he first arrived in Glasgow from Inverness. I've known 'Oleg' since he was a kid.

Mark Kerr also came in, while McCall allowed the likes of Comber, Danny Griffin, Jamie Buchan, Jim Hamilton and Derek Lilley to leave. But, despite all the changes, I was still McCall's captain at first and we steered clear of relegation again that season, finishing above Motherwell, who went down.

Unfortunately, I was suspended for the first game of McCall's first proper season, 2003/04. We played Hibs at home, but I had been sent off near the end of the previous campaign for a handball in the derby against Dundee.

We battered Hibs that day, and it was Del and young Kerr who were McCall's central midfielders. We should have been 6–0 up at half-time but were only leading 1–0.

In the second half, Paterson did his cruciate and Oleg was sent off. We eventually lost 2–1, with Tam McManus scoring a penalty late on. It wasn't the start McCall was looking for with his new-look side, but we soon picked up and I played most of the games early on.

Slowly but surely, though, I could see things unravelling for me under McCall. He had decided to make Del captain, which I was absolutely fine about. I've always known that Del was better captain material than me. I agreed with the decision. More worryingly, I always got the impression that McCall preferred McInnes and Kerr as his favoured duo in the middle of the park. Now, I'm sorry, Del is one of my best mates in the game and Mark is a great guy – but better footballers than me? I don't think so. Not in a million years.

I was a bit pissed off. It came to a head with McCall one day when we all were sitting at the Gussie, an artificial pitch just across from Tannadice that we used for training, in November 2003. While McCall was speaking, I must have said something to one of the other boys. I wasn't intentionally being rude, but he stopped what he was saying and said, 'Shut the fuck up, I'm speaking.' Cally was a bit like that: he liked to show he was in charge at times. His persona at that time was: 'I'm the man.'

I had a go back at him and said, 'Who are you talking to, you fat bastard?'

Now, I know that's not the way you should speak to your manager. But, as much as I liked a lot of McCall's methods, I didn't have the same kind or respect for him that I'd had for Alex Smith. He had tried to put me down in front of people before, which I didn't like. He tried to embarrass me and make me look daft that day, which I thought was out of order. I was one of his best, most experienced players.

He then said, 'Can I speak to you in my office?'

I said, 'No problem.'

I went up and he told me I was out of the squad for the game against Celtic the following day at Tannadice.

Now, I know it's not the right attitude to have but I thought, 'Fuck you, then, you will just lose by even more.'

That Celtic team under Martin O'Neill had Henrik Larsson and Chris Sutton in it – they were so strong. And, sure enough, we got battered 5–1, with Sutton getting a hat-trick and Larsson a double. To be honest, I wouldn't have made much difference that day even if I'd played.

McCall also told me the previous day that if I found a new club I could leave on a free transfer at the end of the season. At that time, I still believed 100 per cent that I was Dundee United's best player, but I didn't want to play for him, so I thought, 'Fine.'

When McCall first came to the club, he had seemed to be this ultra-professional guy, trying to make his mark. But slowly, I felt that level of professionalism got less and less. It sounds like a silly example – especially coming from me – but it seemed to start when he introduced cakes and fizzy juice into the changing-room the day before a game. The worst player on a Friday, as voted for by the rest of the squad, had to bring in cakes for everyone the following Friday. And on the Thursday we had this volleying routine, and the last one to score a volley had to bring in the juice. So initially you had McCall, with his wee pair of glasses and tactics board, looking so professional. Then, a few months on, he was coming away with quotes like, 'Make sure you bring those cakes in, with plenty of cream on them.' And with the juice, he'd say, 'None of this Lucozade pish, make sure it's Coke or Irn-Bru.' Even I knew that wasn't exactly ideal the day before a game.

Anyway, I was still training with the first team every day and I was flying. Around January, I was on the bench for a game against Aberdeen at Tannadice. We were losing 2–1 when I came on with just eighteen minutes left. In the 85th minute, I scored a header from a corner to get us level. Then, late on, I got into the box and was brought down for a penalty. Wee Billy Dodds stepped up to score and we won 3–2.

McCall was on the pitch at the end saluting the fans. He was trying to hold my hand up to the crowd as if I was the hero and *he* deserved the credit for putting me on. I told him to fuck off. For weeks, I'd been reduced to being a bit-part player for virtually nothing. The fans couldn't understand why I wasn't playing. Okay, I shouldn't have sworn at him, but in a tough environment like football there will always be arguments and disagreements, and you have to be big enough to accept that.

All of a sudden, after that Aberdeen game, he started using me again and I was doing really well. I played my part in getting us into the top six in the SPL, which had been our aim all along.

McCall was now eager for me to sign a new contract, but I told him there was no danger that I was staying while he was still in charge. I would be a free agent in the summer. I remember he said that he'd take me for a pint to talk it over one day. It was two days before a game. I met him at around 6 p.m. in the pub and by midnight both of us were absolutely blootered. We even got a kebab afterwards on the way home. He thought he'd be able to twist me round his little finger and I'd sign. But there was no way I was staying, I had made up my mind.

I told him that I had a great chance to sign for the Spanish club Levante, and by that stage, I wanted away from Scottish football. I had been made aware of Levante's interest and, in my mind, I had 95 per cent signed for them and I was looking at a new chapter in my career in Spain. I had always wanted to play abroad and we'd agreed all the terms – a nice £7,000-a-week deal. But it fell through at the last minute, through no fault of my own. Looking back, I should have stayed at United, and I regret not signing a new deal.

Gal was also playing really well in goal and McCall was desperate for us both to sign. I think if we had, United would have finished in the top three of the SPL the following season. Because, as much as it pains me to say it, McCall was getting there with United, along with Chis and Tony – they were building a decent squad. But losing Gal to Norwich City and myself to Brann Bergen were huge blows to him. I don't think he ever recovered from that, because within months of the start of the following season, he was sacked by Thompson.

Listen, on football terms, I liked McCall and nine times out of ten we actually got on fine. But he scared the life out of the young boys at United with his behaviour and I never like to see that. That's where I thought his man-management was really poor.

Overall, I really enjoyed my time at the club. We didn't have the best players in the world, but what a great bunch of lads we had there. We had some good laughs, none more so than when my good mate from Castlemilk, Andy McLaren, came back to the club for a second spell.

Andy had won the Scottish Cup with United in 1994 and is rightly regarded as a legend up there. I'll never forget the day he re-signed in 2003. He was upstairs signing a contract. Now, I don't know what his wages were but, just for argument's sake, let's say he agreed a £2,000-a-week deal with £1,000 appearance money. Andy then walked downstairs into the changing-room and met all the boys, before McCall came in and said he had to speak to the entire squad. Eddie Thompson followed him into the room, so we knew something was wrong. Eddie had just come from his meeting with Andy.

He said, 'Boys, it would really help the club if you could defer all your appearance money until the end of the season.'

You should have seen Andy's face. It was hilarious. He couldn't believe it. He was thinking, 'I've just left Kilmarnock to come back and sign a contract with £1,000 appearance money!' Andy thought they were taking the piss – but it was true.

He'd been at United during the famous Jim McLean era. Well, it was infamous for young players being on shit wages then, and Andy was part of that. He must have been saying to himself, 'I was here for ten years on garbage money. I come back and now you're taking my appearance money off me!'

To be fair, Eddie was as good as his word. The boys deferred, but we got every penny back at the end of the campaign. It actually gave us decent holiday money in the summer, so we weren't complaining too much.

Eddie sadly passed away in October 2008, and I only have good things to say about him as a person. He was a great man. I thought his only mistake as chairman/owner was sacking Alex and Heggy when he did. But he had an idea that McCall was Scottish football's brightest young manager, which was fine. Unfortunately for him, it didn't quite work out like that.

I had played well for United during my time there. In fact, I'd say that some of my best performances in Scottish football came in a tangerine shirt. That brings me back to my lack of international recognition while I was there – and my one and only cap for Scotland.

First of all, let me take you back to my Under-21 days.

I was a regular in the Scotland Under-21 side when I first broke into the Rangers team, and the highlight of my time with them was undoubtedly in 1996 when we reached the semi-final of the European Championships. I was nineteen at the start of the Euro qualifying campaign and Tommy Craig was our manager. We had a really good squad.

Our keepers were Derek Stillie and Colin Meldrum. We had

Jackie McNamara, Scott Marshall, Steven Pressley, Christian Dailly and Stephen Glass in defence. There was myself, Neil Murray, Simon Donnelly and Allan Johnston in midfield, with the likes of Stevie Crawford up front. Every single one of that side went on to play first-team football for their clubs – and most featured for the A squad – which is quite unusual for a Scotland Under-21 group.

We, along with Spain, Italy and France, made it to the last four of the Euros, which was a brilliant achievement for the boys. The semi-finals were normally two-legged affairs, but that year they changed the format and both ties were to be played in one host country, which happened to be Spain – who were our opponents.

We played the Spaniards in front of a huge crowd, near 50,000, in the Olympic Stadium, Espanyol's ground. We were beaten 2–1 and I played really well. The Spanish were a different class and they had the likes of Raúl – who would go on to become a Real Madrid legend – and Iván de la Peña in their line-up. De la Peña scored a great free kick to beat us, but people who were there say I outplayed him that night. All I'll say is I know I played really well – I was pleased with my performance.

France lost to Italy, who had Francesco Totti, Alessandro Nesta and Fabio Cannavaro in their side, in the other semi-final. Cesare Maldini was the Italians' coach. The French had Patrick Vieira, Claude Makélélé, Robert Pirès and Sylvain Wiltord in their squad. All of these guys went on to lift World Cups and Euro Championships for their countries. But, at that time, Scotland were competing with them. It was an incredibly good standard.

In the third/fourth-place play-off, France beat us 1–0, but we had run them and the Spaniards very close. Italy beat Spain in the final to be crowned European champions.

Playing in those types of games didn't faze me, because at that time I was playing with world-class players at Rangers like Laudrup, Durrant and Hateley. I thought I'd play in games like that all my life. I suppose I got a bit complacent. It was like cup finals: I played in one for Rangers and thought I'd have another twenty.

But the Spain game was huge, looking back. I didn't realise it at the time, but a lot of people took notice of my performance against de la Peña, who was regarded as one of Europe's most highly rated youngsters. I swapped shirts with him and I've still got it at home now.

I'd never say I was as good as him. He should probably have done better in his career for the ability he had, even though he went on to play for Barcelona. But I was better than him that night.

He was a great lad as well. It was the summer, so it was holiday time, and we all went out together after the tournament for a night out. Even the likes of Christian Dailly, a model pro, went out, because for a lot of our boys it was their last time in a Scotland squad together. We hooked up with the likes of Raúl and de la Peña, who were brilliant with us. That was an unbelievable time for me.

Now, obviously none of the boys were expecting to be paid for taking Scotland so far in the competition. We were all just delighted to be playing for our country. But it summed up the SFA – and our luck – that the incentive bonus they'd put in place meant that if we finished third, we were due £750. Second would have got us £1,000 and if we'd won it, we'd have got £3,000. Unfortunately, we finished fourth and didn't get a penny!

I loved playing for Scotland; I was always really proud to play for my country. But throughout my time with the national team, I just felt the SFA treated us like kids. I know we were young players, but we weren't children.

I recall we had a double-header in Estonia and Latvia. Remember, at that time the Under-21s played against identical countries as the full squad. Our qualification group mirrored theirs. We travelled with the A squad and usually played the night before them. This was the famous match in Estonia in

October 1996, when the hosts didn't turn up and Scotland kicked off the match with no opposition before walking off the pitch. The chant 'there's only one team in Tallinn' was born that night. I was actually supposed to be on the bench for the full squad because of a few injuries, but I'd picked up a knock myself in the Under-21 game, which put paid to that.

Anyway, the Under-21s were staying in a £10-a-night hotel with loads of Scotland supporters. We then had to take a forty-five-minute bus journey to the hotel where the full squad were staying, for our lunch and dinner. How fucking ridiculous is that? At that time, most of our boys were playing first-team football at clubs like Rangers, Aberdeen and Hearts. But the SFA were treating us like that. It was just bizarre. Why couldn't they just have put us all into the same hotel?

Tommy Craig wasn't necessarily a bad guy and he actually made me captain of the Under-21s after the Euro semi-final defeat to Spain. Sadly, the relationship didn't go too well after that, though, and I don't think he ever forgave me for an incident after a game against Austria in August 1996.

The full squad were playing the Austrians the night after the Under-21s had played them, and drew 0–0. It was a rubbish game, but we had to sit and watch it. Some of the boys, including myself, were sitting playing cards in the middle of the game and the management didn't like it. They thought we should have been tuned into the match, but it was shite. I think from that moment on, Tommy got a bit fed up with me. And I did wonder if he was in Walter Smith's ear at every opportunity telling him bad things about me.

As captain of the Under-21s, I'd often ask him if the boys could go for a beer after games, but he was having none of it. I always wanted to play for Scotland, but after the Spain game in the Euros, when that squad split up, I felt we had gone as far as we could with Tommy as manager.

The players who came in after that were nowhere near as

talented. No disrespect, but I remember we had a guy called Ian McCarron playing who was at Clyde. Boys from Clyde shouldn't be playing for Scotland Under-21s unless they're exceptional.

When Tommy eventually stopped picking me I probably thought – even that early in my career – that I wouldn't win many full caps. Scotland weren't exactly renowned for throwing young players into the side. We never have been, even though every other country in the world seems to do it. And when have the SFA ever picked anyone who would challenge them on anything they did? It's a bit different now, but that's the way it was back then.

I was a bit of a pest to them and they didn't like it. But I could play. However, at times I felt I had too much flair for the way Tommy wanted to play anyway. I'm sure it was my first ever cap for the Under-21s when he stuck me out on the right wing, with Jamie Fullarton in the centre, my position. I was playing in Rangers' first team at the time. Walter and Archie came to watch and the next day they were winding me up in training, giving me pelters, because they knew I hated playing out wide.

I don't think Tommy fancied me, full stop. People on the outside of the game maybe have this perception of me as being a trouble-maker, but I'd refute that. I'm confident that if you asked any of the players I played with, I don't think you'd get one who'd say I was a bad person or that I was a problem in the dressing-room.

In any case, I was surprised when I did get my first full Scotland cap, while at United. It was a 1–1 draw against Poland on Wednesday 25 April 2001 – just five months after I'd arrived from Watford.

To this day, I think there must have been an epidemic in Scottish football and that's why I got a call-up. I'm convinced that nobody else wanted to go to Poland for a friendly, so Andy McLaren, John O'Neil, Kenny Miller and I were called in for it. Before then, when I'd first broken into the Rangers team, I had no complaints about not getting picked for Scotland. A few people in the media thought I deserved a chance because of the impact I'd made at Ibrox, but Scotland had a right good side back then and midfield was their strongest area. There were players like Gary McAllister, Paul McStay, John Collins, Stuart McCall, Eoin Jess, Craig Burley, Ian Ferguson and Ian Durrant vying for spaces. That Craig Brown era was strong. We probably didn't realise it at the time, but we were. We were hard to beat, that's for sure. So I was delighted when Craig picked me for Poland, irrespective of the circumstances.

It was one of his last squads, before Berti Vogts came in. I was actually suspended for Dundee United's game against St Mirren that weekend, and I think that's another reason why I got in. Alex Smith had also been pushing me for a while. To be fair to him, he couldn't believe I wasn't getting a cap. I thought it might be the only one I'd ever get, so I went to Poland. And I was right!

I played fifty-six minutes on the right of a three-man midfield in a 3-5-2 formation. Again, I wasn't used in a position where I could really hurt the opposition. I was asked to do a defensive shift that night as well, which I didn't enjoy. But it was brilliant that Andy and I were on the same trip, two Castlemilk boys. We always joke that myself, Andy and Kenny Dalglish have 103 caps between us: Kenny has 102 and me and Andy have one between us.

I played fifty-six minutes and Andy came on at half-time. We were only on the pitch for ten minutes together. It was funny because when Scott Booth was brought down for Scotland's penalty that night, Andy had the ball in his hands, ready to take it. I was off the pitch at that point. I was desperate for him to take it. I wanted him to score for Scotland, because it would have been great for him. But Booth ran up to Andy and said, 'Craig said I've to hit the penalties.' Incredibly, Andy gave him the ball. It was a friendly and it was Andy's first cap. If it was me, I'd never have given Booth the ball. If he'd said that to me, I'd have said, 'Tell Craig to fuck off, I'm hitting it.' Booth acted like a kid at school, as if it was his ball and no one else was to get it.

I knew after the Poland game that it would definitely be my last cap under Craig. I didn't even play well in the game, if I'm honest. The pitch was heavy and Poland were a pretty decent outfit. I barely got a kick. No, the only gripe I've ever really had with not being picked for Scotland was when Vogts took over – and seemed to cap *everyone* bar me.

I was playing in Dundee derbies during my time at United, and back then they were really good games. I was running the show in some of those matches and was really proud of my performances. Berti hadn't long been appointed as Scotland manager when he came to watch one of them. I'm sure it was a 1–0 victory for us at Dens Park in April 2002.

I was directly up against Gavin Rae, who was playing in central midfield for Dundee. Now, I love big Gavin as a guy. My mate from Australia, Mark Robertson, is married to Gavin's sister-in-law. But that day, I absolutely battered him. I gave him a doing. He couldn't get near me in the middle of the park, and we ran out deserved winners. But a few days later, Berti named his Scotland squad: I wasn't in it – but Gavin was!

I don't know what game he was watching at Dens, but I'm sure Berti must have thought Gavin was me. I played really well that day. I couldn't believe he'd picked the one-eyed fish before me! Seriously, I think I must have been the only Scottish player alive not to get a cap under Berti – he was handing them out like confetti.

I think back now and there were guys like Gary Holt, Robbie Stockdale and Scott Dobie getting caps ahead of me. How the fuck did that happen? I'm not sure if Tommy Burns, who was Berti's assistant, didn't like me or if he'd been fed bad info from Tommy Craig, who was a good friend of Burns. For a spell at United, I was in the best form I'd been in since breaking through at Rangers.

I think I deserved more caps under Berti. No disrespect, but I was better than guys like Stockdale and Dobie, every day of the week. Yet Berti never once even spoke to me about a call-up. Alex Smith and I couldn't believe it. And by then I really wanted to be in the squad. I could see everyone else getting in and I was thinking, 'What do I need to do to get picked here?'

If Berti had, I'd have played in a few big games for Scotland. Berti took us to the Euro 2004 play-off against Holland, for example. We beat the Dutch 1–0, thanks to James McFadden's goal, before getting hammered 6–0 in Amsterdam.

I felt I could have offered the team something different. Aside from Faddy, who was a bit of a maverick, all we had was runners and workers in the attacking third. I believe I could have created chances for Scotland and given us a different dimension – even coming off the bench. But it wasn't to be for me at international level, despite the four and a half good years at Dundee United. I loved it there and the fans were great with me. I even made it into Lorraine Kelly's greatest-ever United team, so I'll take that.

As I've already said, the Levante deal never happened for me. Bizarrely, I heard that Steve Archibald was asked by the Spaniards about me. If so, I've no idea what he'd have said or, indeed, if he knew too much about me, but whoever they spoke to and for whatever the reasons, the deal was dead.

I was devastated because I thought Spanish football would have suited my game down to the ground and the lifestyle was very appealing.

United were still desperate to keep me, but I wanted a change. I just didn't think that a change would mean a switch to Norway.

10

FOREIGN ADVENTURES

I KNEW as much as most people in Scotland about SK Brann Bergen before I signed for them. The former Aberdeen and Dundee United striker Robbie Winters played for them, and that was about it. Even then, I didn't know Robbie too well anyway. I was heading into the unknown for my first taste of football abroad.

Bergen itself is on the west coast of Norway. It has a population of around 250,000 people and is the second-biggest city in the country behind Oslo. SK Brann hadn't won the Norwegian title since 1963 and that's why the likes of Robbie and I were brought in, to try to end Rosenborg's dominance of the championship.

I was up for a new challenge, and this was it. I signed in the summer of 2004, after finishing up at Tannadice, so I hadn't even started doing pre-season training yet. But, of course, when I arrived at Brann, they were bang in the middle of their domestic campaign.

After my first training session with them, I remember thinking to myself, 'Holy fuck, these boys are fit.' Our manager was a guy called Mons Ivar Mjelde, who had been a striker at the club in his playing days. He had five years as Brann gaffer and is now coaching the Norwegian side Start.

Right from the off, I knew I wasn't Mons's signing. It was the sporting director, Per-Ove Ludvigsen, who had brought me to the club – which was common practice at clubs on the continent.

Mons and I would go on to have a fiery relationship, but, ultimately, he was a good guy. He was a family man who had the club at heart. We just didn't see eye to eye when it came to football very often. Anyway, when I arrived in Bergen, I convinced myself that I had a newfound freedom and I could go out into town and no one there would know who I was. I couldn't have been more wrong. As usual, I was naive.

Initially, I was staying in a Scandic hotel and I was bored out my skull, right from the off. So I did the only thing I knew how to in that situation – headed out for a smoke and a few beers. But the following day, I was called in by Per-Ove, who had already been filled in on what I'd been up to.

He said, 'Charlie, you can't just stroll into the town, smoke cigarettes and drink beer.' I asked him how he knew where I'd been and he explained that in the town of Bergen, no one supported anyone other than SK Brann. That's when the penny dropped. It's a bit like Newcastle in that sense. So, everyone would have known who I was. I must say that the fans were terrific with me right away. We had around 20,000 at our home games most weeks, which was excellent.

So that was the end of my stay at the Scandic hotel. I had only been there a matter of days and, essentially, Per-Ove told me that I couldn't stay on my own – Caroline and the kids hadn't moved over at this point. It didn't take him long to work me out! So I was out of the hotel. I ended up being taken in by the former Aberdeen player Cato Guntveit, who is a bit of a club legend at Brann. He put me up in his spare room.

Robbie Winters only had a two-bedroom house then, and his missus, April, was due another baby at that time, so I couldn't stay with him for long. I was only with Cato for a few months, but it probably felt like about ten years for him.

For me, I was just enjoying a change of scenery, somewhere new and different, and Bergen is a brilliant city. It has a laid-back feel about it that I enjoyed. It was different to Glasgow in that sense, but it was similar in that I couldn't really go out unnoticed for a few bevvies. In fact, by the end of my stay in Norway I could barely go out in Bergen without being mobbed by supporters. It got a bit ridiculous, and it's because it's a one-team city.

People often ask me about the standard of football in Norway and I tell them it was good. If you take Rangers and Celtic out of the equation, it's very similar to the Scottish game. I remember around that time that Rangers struggled to beat Molde in the UEFA Cup, and they're a decent Norwegian side, nothing more. Most of the time Brann played against them, we battered them. So the standard was pretty decent.

As I said, Mons was a really nice guy away from the ground. But in terms of tactics and team selection? In my opinion, he didn't have a fucking clue. And sadly for Mons, the fans liked me more than they liked him.

The fans seemed to take me to their hearts right away. Scoring a hat-trick against Rosenborg, which I did a year later, in June 2005, also helped with my popularity. I've still got the match ball from that game. After that, I could do no wrong in the eyes of the supporters. We'd beaten the top team in Norway 4–1 at home and I'd run riot. The supporters were demanding that I get a new contract after the match.

I scored a penalty before Rosenborg equalised, but I hit another one before half-time, then Raymond Kvisvik made it 3–1. I wrapped it up towards the end for my first hat-trick in senior football. There's a cracking picture of me being lifted by my team-mate Paul Scharner, the Austrian defender who went on to play for Wigan and West Brom in the Premier League.

From the start, though, they liked me because they saw me getting stuck in. It didn't bother me who we were playing against or which players I was taking on. I think they saw me as a bit of a maverick. I was someone who played off the cuff and who could create chances in the final third.

We signed a lad called Bengt Saeternes up front, who was a great guy. We were really tight and became good pals. Bengt and Robbie were the club's two main strikers and both of them were flying. They worked really well together in attack and scored a lot of goals for Brann, but Mons decided to throw a major spanner in the works by deciding to play just one forward up top, with me as a wide right attacker. That often meant dropping Robbie to the bench. I hate playing wide right, I have done my entire career, but for some reason Mons just refused to play me in central midfield.

We had Kvisvik on the left-hand side, and what a footballer that boy was. His ability was frightening at times. Unfortunately, Raymond was as bad as me when it came to drinking and gambling. He was nuts. That's why I liked him.

We had our captain, Martin Andresen, in the middle of the park and, contrary to what people believed in Bergen, we got on really well together. Everyone in Norway seemed to think we'd had a fall-out because he was playing centrally ahead of me, but that was crazy, just not true. Granted, I was stuck on the right wing and I didn't like it, but that wasn't Martin's fault.

I remember playing Molde away from home in a league game and I scored around the 50th-minute mark to put us 1–0 up. By fifty-five minutes, my number was up on the board and Mons was taking me off. The fans could tell I wasn't best pleased, and neither were they. I looked at him as I came off as if to say, 'Are you for fucking real?' But he wouldn't budge and it was a bit of a love-hate relationship we had.

In my third season, 2006, we were ten points clear at the top of the league but started to let it slip. A few of the boys seemed to lose their nerve. Their bottle was crashing a bit, and Mons just didn't know how to change things. I said to him one day, 'Mons, you have to change the team; some of the boys are playing poorly.'

He held a meeting between the players and everyone said

their piece. So what do you think he did for the next game? He dropped me out of the side and kept the rest of it the same! I couldn't fucking believe it.

In the local newspapers the following day, Cato told me the headlines were all about how I didn't want to play and had pulled myself out of the squad. That was total bullshit, but Mons was trying to shift the blame on to me for the team's collapse.

Our lead was being cut by Rosenborg all the time. It was down to two points and we were playing Stabaek on a Monday night, away from home. We were winning 1–0, through a good finish from Robbie. I was on the bench along with the skipper, Martin, who'd been binned in favour of new signing Eirik Bakke, the ex-Leeds United midfielder.

Mons turned to one of the other subs and told him to get stripped, but then, with about six minutes to go, Stabaek equalised. So instead, he turned to me and told me I was going on. I wasn't too happy, but I wanted to try to prove him wrong. It was the last minute and a cross found me at the far edge of the box. I've chested it and hit a volley that bulleted in off the post. What a fucking strike it was! We'd won it 2–1 and as I celebrated I made sure I ran right past Mons on my way towards the Brann fans.

I was getting texts from people in Bergen for days afterwards telling me how much they loved me. That was a strange thing over there. The punters seemed to be able to get hold of your mobile number and wouldn't think twice about giving you a call or sending a text after a match. It was bizarre.

We still ended up blowing the title and allowing Rosenborg to win it by six points, but it's weird in Norway – when you're second you get a silver medal and the clubs celebrate it. I remember we held a 'silver medal ceremony' after our victory over Ham-Kam in October 2006. They actually wanted us to do a lap of honour for finishing second. I was having none of that. The way I was brought up at Rangers, you never celebrate being second best.

I walked straight off the pitch, refusing to take part in it, and in for a shower. The kit man came in and said, 'Charlie, you have to come out and celebrate.' But I told him there was no way I was going to parade around the pitch. How can you be happy about letting the league championship slip out of your grasp? I gave him my medal and told him to keep it.

I knew we'd have won that title if it hadn't been for Mons making an arse of it. Robbie felt the same way, but he's a quiet guy so didn't say too much. Unlike me, he didn't want to rock the boat with Mons. He kept himself to himself.

Anyway, Caroline and the kids had come over and we bought a house in Bergen, after my stint at Cato's house. We settled there as a family and it was a nice lifestyle. My brother and uncles came over all the time – they loved the place. But by God, I was bored a lot of the time. I missed Glasgow a bit and at times I yearned for my mates.

Most of the time, it was just pure boredom. There were times when we'd train at 6 p.m. on a Sunday night, up in the mountains, when we couldn't see a yard in front of us. Bergen's title is 'the City of the Seven Mountains'. That wasn't for me, and it got to the stage when I wanted out of there.

Mons was in charge for my full two and a half years there. And as soon as I left, Brann won the league! You really couldn't make it up. But I was proud of what I achieved in Norway. I won the 2004 Norwegian Cup shortly after I joined – albeit coming on as a late sub for Robbie in a 4–1 victory after he'd scored and Bengt helped himself to a hat-trick. I can look myself in the mirror and know I played well for Brann. I think the regard in which the fans still hold me speaks volumes for how I performed. I definitely felt I did myself justice over there.

The fans adored me because I could play. And I'd battle for the ball on the pitch as well, which isn't really a trait associated with most of the Norwegian boys. Our local rivals were Vålerenga, who had a player called Ardian Gashi. He was actually a Kosovan, but he spent most of his career playing in Norwegian football. He eventually signed for Brann. The fans of Brann and Vålerenga hated each other, so while he was playing for Vålerenga I used to kick the shit out of him. He wasn't just one of their key players; he was the guy who got them going, but I wasn't going to shy away from him.

There was one game where I had him with the throat at one point. The Brann punters loved that. They detested wee Ardian, yet he came to us in 2006 for a year. I just didn't give a fuck and that's what the crazy punters liked most about me. To be honest, and I don't want to sound too big-headed, but I think they were also surprised they had me after what I'd achieved in Scotland. I got the impression that they believed they were lucky to have me there. But SK Brann are a great club run by wonderful people. They couldn't have done enough for me and my family over there, and I'll never forget that.

Something I'll also never be allowed to forget is being 'punk'd' on Norwegian TV. If you check YouTube now, you'll see me in all my glory being caught out, big-time. *Punk'd* is a huge show over in Norway and originates from the American programme of the same name, the one Ashton Kutcher used to present.

Obviously, I was quite a well-known character over there, so I was a prime target. It was my team-mates who put them up to it – only because I was constantly doing things to them in the dressing-room. I'd get up to all sorts with pranks and practical jokes, but I was undoubtedly the victim this time. Andresen and a few others were behind it, the bastards.

I was duped into thinking my car was being lifted by the police in relation to a nearby crime. As part of the ruse, they even got guys in balaclavas to speed past me shouting my name. I totally bought it. At first, I was a bit wary and I thought something wasn't right. Then when I saw my car being towed away on the back of a truck, I started to believe it was really happening. I didn't have Norwegian TV at home, so I didn't know anything about the programme. That's why I fell for it, hook, line and sinker.

It's funny watching it on YouTube now. I have to hold my hands up; they done me a cracker, fair play to them.

As a family, we really took the club and Bergen to our hearts. My daughter Demi can still speak fluent Norwegian and my son Jordan was diagnosed with dyslexia while he was in Bergen, and the club were very helpful to us. Both of them started in International School, before moving to normal Norwegian schools. I used to see them trudging away to school in the snow every morning; I can still picture them now.

The winters were crazy in Norway. Blizzards, heavy snow, ice, freezing cold, you name it – we experienced it. It was much worse than anything we were used to in Scotland. But when I think back, they were good times. They were happy times with my family that I'll always treasure. I probably didn't appreciate them while I was there, but I do now.

In the end, I just needed something different at the end of 2006. It's difficult to put my finger on it. I got itchy feet and wanted to play somewhere else. Maybe the football over there lacked something – a bit of spark. The constant disagreements with Mons over what position I should be playing in didn't help either. A few of the fans weren't too happy with me when I left, because I slaughtered him in the press. But I think most of them still love me. I have a lot of Brann followers on Twitter, for example, and I'm sure I'll always be welcomed back.

Even though I was outspoken at times, I think most people connected with the club respected me for being honest and forthright. As I've said, I had nothing against Mons as a guy. He was a good man with a lovely family that I met on several occasions. I just didn't think he knew too much about football. In my opinion, we had a team at Brann who were good enough to win that Norwegian title every year. Maybe that came to fruition when I left, but during my time there, we lost games against poor opposition due to poor decisions.

I have to admit that a lot of the time I felt, 'I'm better than this,

I should be playing at a higher level.' And I had got fit over in Norway, proper fit. I became more disciplined there. I wasn't out as much as I'd been in Scotland. Of course, I had my blow-outs and I'd get absolutely blootered at times. I'd still have the odd two-day session. Robbie and I would get the families together if it was a nice day and we'd have a barbecue and a few drinks. That's normally how a bender started.

I have to say, Robbie was like a woman, though. I'd be having a few beers, watching the football and he'd be sitting with Caroline and April having a cup of tea. He'll love me for saying that!

But for most of the time I was really fit, as fit as I'd been at any point in my career. And that's why, in January 2007, I was delighted when John Viola got me back in at Rangers to train at Murray Park.

Walter was back in charge for his second stint at the club and no one was supposed to know that I was training with them for a week. You have to understand, it was a dream for me to go back to Rangers. I loved every minute of it. This time, I was older, wiser, a bit more mature – and I was flying. I was as fit as a fiddle and I saw it as a golden opportunity for me. That's why I barely told a soul. I didn't want to jeopardise any potential move back to Ibrox.

But big Derek Johnstone, the former Rangers striker turned radio pundit, let it slip on air that he believed Charlie Miller was going to re-sign for Rangers that week. I hadn't told D.J., I hadn't told anyone. But God, I played well that week, I know I did.

Every day, players like Barry Ferguson and Kris Boyd would joke with me, asking: 'Have you signed that contract yet?' But I was taking nothing for granted because, remember, I knew Walter.

I had done really well, but on the Thursday, I phoned JV and asked him to give Walter a call. I wanted him to gauge whether or not I'd be offered a deal. If it wasn't on the cards, I didn't want to go in on the Friday. It was coming towards the end of the transfer window and Brann had agreed to release me from my contract, so I was on tenterhooks a bit. I was desperate to sign. But I wasn't keen on going into Murray Park on my last day to get a knock-back from Walter and then have to say goodbye to all the boys. So John phoned him and the feedback was good. Walter said he wanted to speak to me on the Friday.

In my head, I was thinking, 'He's going to give me a six-month contract, from January to June. Why else would he want me in?' I was trying not to get too excited, but I had convinced myself that it was on. After leaving the club, when I didn't really want to before, I felt I had unfinished business at Rangers.

So I went in the next day and finished training. Still, Walter hadn't said anything to me. In the corridor, he was standing with Coisty and Kenny McDowall and I said, 'Gaffer, can I speak to you?'

Walter said: 'Aye, no problem, come into the office.'

I went to sit down at his desk and before my arse had even hit the chair, he said, 'The answer's no.'

I was fucking devastated. Genuinely, I had a tear in my eye that day. I thought I was getting a six-month contract and a dream return to Rangers. Instead, I was out on my ear again. I couldn't have envisaged Walter doing that to me, offering me absolutely nothing, after the week I'd had in training. I didn't think he'd be as cruel as that.

I didn't even ask him why. Thinking back, I'm surprised I didn't fly off the handle. It's in my nature to say, 'Why the fuck not?' But I think I was so stunned that I just walked out of the room.

One thing I'd never done during my time at Ibrox previously was give Walter cheek, or attempt to argue with him. I didn't even do that when I was eighteen or nineteen, so I wasn't about to start now.

It was a strange episode, I just couldn't get my head around it. That hurt me, it really did. That was as low as I've ever felt in my life, not just in football. It's the worst feeling I've ever had. I was as low as a snake's belly, as Gazza would say.

It would have meant so much for me to go back there. But to this day, I don't know Walter's reasons for it. It was as if he'd woken up after a bad sleep the night before and taken it out on me, because when he'd spoke to JV the night before, it looked like I'd be signing.

Maybe, then, was it the chairman's influence? If I'm being honest, I think David Murray might have put the block on it. Big Alex McLeish has told me before that while he was Rangers manager between 2001 and 2006, he tried to sign me twice and, on both occasions, Murray said no. I don't know why he would hold a grudge against me, but I don't think he's ever liked me and I've never liked him.

I've never spoken about it before, but I can say what I think now. He's from Edinburgh and I think, in his eyes, I was just a 'weegie Ned'. I reckon that's what he thought of me.

Wee Barry had been running me in and out of training all that week, as I'd been staying at my uncle Benny's house in Bishopbriggs. I remember getting into Barry's Range Rover that day and barely saying a word to him. I didn't have to – he could see how upset I was. Barry didn't really know what to say. It was a shame, because I got the impression that Barry quite fancied having me alongside him in Rangers' midfield – something we'd rarely done before. I think myself, playing in front of Barry, with him feeding me in positions where I could hurt the opposition, would have been brilliant. But it wasn't to be.

If I'd have got that second chance at Rangers, I'd never have been as daft as I was the first time. I just know I wouldn't. I'd have screwed the nut and taken the opportunity I'd been given.

After the move fell through, I had a fall-out with JV and Phil McTaggart, who works alongside him as an agent. That was my fault. I was ignorant. JV had been my agent for years and was best man at my wedding. But I signed for the Belgian side

Lierse without even speaking to them about it. Neil Murray, my ex-team-mate at Rangers, was now an agent himself, and he set the deal up for me.

Neil had told me that he'd spoken to JV and was halving the deal with him. So I thought everything was fine and just went ahead with it, instead of picking the phone up to John and asking if it was true, which it wasn't entirely. There had been a mix-up in communication, but instead of sorting it I did nothing. My head was still all over the place after the rejection from Rangers. But I still feel bad about it because Phil especially was working his balls off for me, trying to get me out of Norway. I had six months left on my contract at Brann and he helped persuade the club to mutually terminate. JV wasn't too happy, but I had to get on with signing for Lierse and starting yet another new chapter in my career.

11

BELGIUM TO BRISBANE

LIKE WITH Brann, I knew very little about Lierse other than the fact that Pieter Huistra used to play for them. Kjetil Rekdal, who had been manager at Brann's big rivals Vålerenga, had always liked me when I played in Norway and he was now manager of Lierse. But when I arrived in Belgium, the club were in an impossible situation – even worse than when I signed for Dundee United. They were rock bottom of the league and I had only signed a short-term deal until the summer. I started reasonably well, but we ended up losing the relegation play-off and we went down.

In the close season, I should have signed for Kaiserslautern in the Bundesliga 2, Germay's second tier. Rekdal had moved there and wanted to take me with him, but no one at Lierse informed me of this. Weeks later, Rekdal came out publicly and questioned my ambition. He couldn't believe I was going to re-sign for Lierse in the Belgian second division, instead of going to Germany. He presumed I was being offered sacks of cash from Lierse, but that was rubbish. The real reason was that I didn't know a thing about it. To this day, I've never asked Neil Murray what happened to that deal.

Lierse offered me a new contract almost immediately after we'd gone down and, stupidly, I signed. It was rushed and I was an idiot to commit to them so early on in pre-season, especially after being relegated, but my head was fucked by that point. I was still hurting from the Rangers fiasco and I just wasn't thinking straight. I ended up signing a three-year deal with Lierse, which seems amazing now. They wanted me to help the club bounce straight back into the top flight.

I wasn't on great money, but at that time in Belgium, you were only taxed 18 per cent on your earnings. However, in the September, just a month after the new season started, that tax for footballers was going to rise to 50 per cent – and I had no idea! It had been announced by the Belgian government the year before, but I was clueless. I remember looking at my wages one day and saying to Benny, the guy who dealt with the finances at the club, 'I've not been paid the right money.' Half of my wages weren't there. But Benny was adamant that my wage slip was correct.

This was a club who, when they originally signed me, told me days later that they might not be able to pay me. Lierse had major financial problems before the Egyptian businessman Maged Samy came in as owner.

Benny told me about the government changing the tax from 18 to 50 per cent, but I was having none of it. They'd known this almost a year before but got me to sign a new contract in the summer, following relegation, and didn't think to tell me about it. Not a fucking chance. I had taken a drop in wages to sign in the first place because we'd gone down a division.

I was living on my own in Belgium, while my wife and kids were back in Glasgow. I was supposed to be supporting them. I told Benny I couldn't live on that wage, and it was such a shame, because I'd had a cracking six months at Lierse, despite failing to keep them up.

However, maybe the club's biggest mistake was putting me into a hotel next door to a pub. When I arrived in Belgium at first, I was promised a certain amount of money a month, a luxury apartment and a Kia Sorento Jeep. Instead, on my first day, they told me that they didn't know if they could afford my wages. They gave me a crappy wee Kia and there was no apartment. I was stuck in a hotel, paying for my own food. I couldn't believe it. I was there for a couple of months before I eventually moved in with Cris De Kepper and her husband, Jeff.

Cris had a job at Lierse and decided to take me in. She saw that I was finding it difficult living in a hotel and took pity on me. She and Jeff – who is an Anderlecht fan – are such lovely people and I'll always be grateful for everything they did for me in Belgium. I got to know their family really well. They loved me to bits and the feeling was mutual. They really looked after me.

I still keep in touch with Cris and Jeff, and they come to Glasgow regularly to visit me. I had them over during the World Cup in summer 2014 and we watched the Belgium v USA match in the pub together. I was the first and last player she ever put up. When I left, she was quite upset, and I don't think she ever wanted to feel like that again by taking any more players in.

In the dressing-room at Lierse, former Belgian international Bob Peeters – who is now manager of Charlton Athletic – and goalkeeper Nico Vaesan were the other experienced pros in there. A lot of the boys spoke Flemish and I felt a bit out of it at times. I'd tend to eat and socialise with the younger ones more. My wee mate Bueno Ernandes De Castro from Brazil, was my best pal. Mustapha Jarju from Gambia was another top boy who I got on really well with. The three of us would play cards and have a laugh together.

I played against some top players over there. My first ever game in 2007 was against Standard Liege, who had Marouane Fellaini, Axel Witsel and Steven Defour in their line-up. They're all super-stars now and in the Belgian national team. They also had the American centre-back Oguchi Onyewu, who's been at AC Milan; the Brazilian defender Dante, who is at Bayern Munich; and the ex-Liverpool front-man Milan Jovanovic playing for them. They were a really strong side back then and they beat us 3–2 in that game at their place, with two dodgy penalties – one in the 95th minute. And we weren't even that great. Even then, I wasn't too impressed with Fellaini, who has now flopped at Manchester United, but I liked Witsel a lot – he is now playing in Russia with Zenit St Petersburg and worth upwards of £20 million.

Liege didn't even win the league that year. They were third, with Anderlecht top and they were also a really good side. Their star man was Marcin Wasilewski, who plays with Leicester in the Premier League now. We'd managed to scrape to second bottom in the table, sending Beveren straight down. We then faced a promotion/relegation play-off, which is a group format. The club had survived the same scenario the year before, but not this time. We were favourites but lost out to Mechelen, who went up and we went down.

I should have gone away, kept myself fit and been ready for the challenge of helping them get back up, but, needless to say, I didn't. The problem I had that summer was that I had come back to Glasgow in the close season and, as it was Rangers' tenth year anniversary of nine-in-a-row, Lierse had given me an extra ten days' holiday. I have to admit, I got blitzed every day when I was home. I was just in party mode and couldn't get out of it.

I returned to Belgium for pre-season training really out of shape. I was so unfit it was untrue. And I knew it. Looking back, I actually don't think I've *ever* recovered from that six-week bender. That might be hard for some people to believe, but I'd basically done nothing fitness-wise during that entire time before returning to Lierse, and I had been bevvying hard almost every day. Compared with how I'd been the previous summer at Brann, when I'd gone back to Murray Park, it was night and day.

I wasn't in any fit state to help the team, but, after the tax issue, I was out of there anyway. There was no way I could stay. Maged Samy thought he could buy you with his cash – one-off payments for winning games and incentives like that, but I wasn't having it. He'd given me a poor contract and now I was getting 50 per cent tax taken off me. He told me he'd give me 70 per cent of it back if I got Lierse promoted, and he probably would have, but my heart and mind weren't in it any longer.

In the end, Lierse were happy to get me off the wage bill and it was agreed that I could leave towards the end of that 2007/08 season. When I left, I could have chased them for a lot more than the £30,000 I received, because I had two years left on my contract. But I didn't, which was probably a bit stupid when I think about it now. I just wanted out.

Ian Ferguson, my old Rangers team-mate, had called me out of the blue and offered me the chance to play in Australia's A-League with the Central Coast Mariners. I thought, 'Fuck it, why not?' I told Fergie that I couldn't go for any less than $350,000 a year, as well as a car and a house. I'd told Lierse I was going, but it had to be worth my while to move from Europe to the other side of the world. But when Fergie got back to me, he said they could only offer me half of that.

Thankfully, I'd also got a call from big Craig Moore asking me to go to Brisbane Roar. At first I'd told him no, because I'd given Fergie my word. But when the money wasn't there, I called Oz back and said I'd go. Oz was a key player at Brisbane Roar and they had Frank Farina, the former Australia national coach, as gaffer.

I came back to Glasgow for a fortnight before getting on a plane to go down under. I stayed with Oz for six weeks before Caroline and the kids came over. Oz and his wife and kids are like family to me anyway so it was great. I spoke to Caroline every day for those six weeks and it wasn't a problem.

The lifestyle was magic. We lived in the Gold Coast, which is just stunning. It's the best place I've ever stayed in my career. We had a lovely house and it was perfect for a while. But I probably enjoyed the lifestyle *too* much. That was a problem.

I was drinking far too much in Australia. Myself, Oz, big Boab Malcolm – another ex-Rangers player who joined the club – and Danny Tiatto, the ex-Manchester City and Australia midfielder, would all go out for a bevvy together. I'd also end up meeting people over there and I'd befriend them.

Outside football, my best mate was a guy called Div Duff, from Aberdeen. He's a big Dons fan. I was in the pub one day and he was standing outside having a fag. I asked him for a light and he said, 'You're not that Orange bastard, Charlie Miller, are you?' From then on, we were best mates. Div works offshore and he's a great guy.

When I got to Australia, looking back, I probably knew it was the beginning of the end for me football-wise. Don't get me wrong, we had a good squad at the Roar and I loved Frank as a coach. We all wanted to play for him. In a way, what we had at Brisbane under Frank was probably similar to what Walter had at Rangers with the older boys during the nine-in-a-row era at Ibrox. In terms of team spirit and guys who were willing to give everything for the manager, there were definite comparisons.

I have a lot of respect for Frank and always will have. I felt sorry for him, the way it ended at Brisbane. He lost his job because of a drink-drive charge. I think he was the equivalent of a glass of wine over the limit – and it was from the night before – but he was fired and got a really hard time for it. His good reputation was tarnished, and that was wrong.

The Australian FA had a big hand in his sacking. They wanted him out, and due to Brisbane's financial problems at the time, they were running the club. That didn't help. They were calling the shots. They might have had a big say in me, Craig Moore, Bob Malcolm and Danny Tiatto leaving as well. Because we were the highest earners at Brisbane Roar, it made sense for them to try and force us out once the new boss Ange Postecoglu took over.

When Frank left, my head went again and I knew my time at the club was coming to an end. People think I fell out with Ange, but I didn't. I was willing to give him the benefit of the doubt, even though he'd gone straight from being a TV pundit with Fox Sports to being our gaffer.

It was Greek people who owned the club and I think that played a big part in him getting the job. It didn't help that in his role as an A-League analyst on TV, he'd criticised a lot of our boys. As soon as he came in, he bad-mouthed Oz, which wasn't a great start. Ultimately, Ange wanted rid of the older pros at the club.

Oz left for Greece, Boab came back to Scotland and I wanted out as well. I knew I had the chance to sign for Gold Coast United, which was appealing to me.

In Ange's first game at the Roar, we battered Wellington Phoenix 4–1 and I scored a goal. But I remember him coming in afterwards and saying it wasn't good enough. I was thinking, 'What more does he fucking want?'

To be fair to Ange, he went on to win two grand finals in the A-League and is now the Socceroos' head coach, so he must have something about him. Fair play to him. Ironically, big Oz is now a Socceroos ambassador and works alongside Ange with the national team. They were at the World Cup together in summer 2014 in Brazil.

Anyway, I signed for Gold Coast, which was where I lived anyway, and at first I thought, 'I could settle over here for the rest of my life.' I scored on my debut for the coach Miron Bleiberg, an Israeli. He was a character. Miron thought he was a bit of a football philosopher and he's now managing in Australia's lower leagues.

It seemed to be the perfect move for me at the time, but I had problems in my family life. Caroline and I weren't getting on, and she'd gone home just as I signed for Gold Coast. She was getting fed up with all my drinking and betting – and rightly so.

We were living in Hope Island; the beach was two minutes away, and it should have been sensational for us all. But while I played for the Roar, my average day consisted firstly of getting up at 5 a.m. to go to training in Brisbane – we trained early in the morning because of the heat – along with Oz, Boab and Danny. We'd travel up together, with training starting at 7.30 a.m. and finishing at 9.30 a.m. We'd get back to Gold Coast and then head for our favourite haunt, the Boardwalk. That was like my second home. We could have our lunch in there, there was a pub in it – and there was even an on-site bookie there too. It was manna from heaven for me.

Caroline was working as a carer in an old folks' home. The kids were at school, so I had a bit of free time on my hands. I'd sit in there all day and get half-cut. I don't mind admitting that I was a complete c*** to her during that time. Our relationship wasn't working at all and times weren't good – despite the stunning surroundings. The weather was too good to sit in the house. That was my excuse.

Don't get me wrong, we had some good times in Australia as well. When I had the sensible head on, I'd have a few drinks, go home for the kids coming in from school and then we'd have a barbecue out the back of the house. That was brilliant. The lifestyle in Australia was the best I've ever experienced in my career. But I just wanted to rip the arse out of it.

I regret doing what I did and falling out with Caroline. If I'd have screwed the nut a bit more, stayed off the drink and kept myself fit, I could have had a long career in the A-League. There are some top players playing there now who are well into their late thirties. But I suppose the flip side to that is that I'm a great believer in the adage, if your time's up, it's up. And I'm not daft, I knew I was coming to the end.

My kids were thousands of miles away in Glasgow and I had to come home.

12

DEMONS

I'VE been accused in the past of having a serious drink problem, but I don't. I probably drink a lot more *now* than I ever did when I was playing. When I was a player, I'd always go for a drink on a Saturday night. Then, hands up, I'd enjoy a Super Sunday the following day. And I'd have beer, pizza, kebabs, the lot.

I'd even start an argument with Caroline over nothing, just to get her out of the house. And I'd always go for a drink on a Tuesday with the Rangers boys especially

I don't remember ever being drunk during a game. The closest I got was probably that match for Dundee United against St Johnstone at McDiarmid Park when we were trying to stay up. I don't know how I got through that, and even scored a vital goal. But I've seen what alcohol abuse can do to people. My good pal Andy McLaren had well-documented problems with drink and drugs and I'm full of admiration for how he's come through that.

I've never feared that drink would get a hold of me the way it did with Andy. He's done brilliantly to come back from the brink. I remember going to see him once when he was at Reading and I was at Watford. He was in the midst of his problems, so me, Caroline, JV and my friend and accountant Dave McGee, went to meet him and, I must admit, I really feared for him that day. I was worried about him. He was in a bad way, really rough. I probably didn't help matters. He had just come off the bevvy and I tried to break the ice by asking if he wanted a pint. In hindsight, it wasn't the brightest comment from me, but it was Castlemilk humour and I'm sure Andy appreciated it. The way he's bounced back has been incredible.

I'm drinking a lot these days. And I know that in ten to fifteen years I'll probably still be sitting in Harry's Bar at the King's Park Hotel having a pint with the regulars, Davie, Derek, Mark, Ian, Barry, Brian, Steph, Gordy, Peter and Liz. It's not the most fashionable pub in the world, but it's a wee quiet place where I can be myself and I don't get bothered by anyone. I enjoy it.

I can sit and have a punt as well, watching the football or the racing on the big TVs. Now, gambling *is* a vice that has got a hold of me at certain points in my career and I've found it hard to wrestle myself away from it. This will be the first time I've really spoken about my gambling addiction and not a lot of people will know that I spent two years going to Gamblers Anonymous meetings while I was a player at Dundee United. You can never really put a figure on this type of thing, but, honestly, I've lost around £1 million at the bookies during my career. At least.

I've been a gambler virtually all my life, but when I was at Tannadice between 2000 and 2003, I knew I had a real problem with the betting. I stopped it for two years and didn't have a bet at all while I attended the meetings. It might sound daft, but I wasn't gambling to win money. I was doing it for the rush and buzz I got when my horse got beat by a nose. How stupid is that?

At that time, I had a Gold Card and a Clydesdale Card. Caroline normally had the Clydesdale one, but I'd think nothing of lifting £500 out of the Gold Card and heading to the bookies. It came to a head during my time at United, but it had been building up for years before that. Listen, I starting going into the bookies in Castlemilk before I was even out of school. Whether it was a couple of quid on a horse or a greyhound, or putting on a football coupon at the weekend, I always liked a bet. Obviously it esca-lated when I became a professional footballer and was earning good money, but, my God, I must be the worst gambler in the world. I'm hopeless at it and that's why I ended up in so much bother.

I remember when I was at Watford in 2000, before I'd got to Dundee United, I got a tip from Billy Dodds for a horse that was running in the Cambridgeshire, which is a big race at Newmarket run every September. It was called Katie Nowaitee; I'll never forget it. Billy was right into his horses, so his info was usually bang on. The horse was a huge price at 25/1 – this was weeks before the race. But instead of taking £500 out of the bank and sticking it on at 25/1 or doing £250 each way, I was trying to get a double up. For a month before it had even run, I couldn't get a single winner to go with Katie Nowaitee. I was doing £100 doubles every day but just could not get a horse to win, which would leave me waiting on Katie to win a fortune. It was ridicu-lous. And all of this time, I was losing the price of 25/1, which was going down all the time.

I was trying to get one horse up to leave me with about a grand going on to the Cambridgeshire. Why did I not just bet Katie Nowaitee for a grand single? That shows how bad a gambler I really am. On the day of the Cambridgeshire, my mate John McKenna and his wife came down for the race. I had also told all the Watford boys about Doddsie's tip, so the likes of Neil Cox and others were also on it.

Can you believe that by the day of the race, all I had on it was £90 at a price of 6/1? John had a tenner on it, Coxy had £100 at 7/1. And, needless to say, it fucking stoated home. It had gone from 25/1 to 6/1 and all I was getting back was £630. I could have had it at 25/1 all along.

Because I was so raging, I ended up blowing the £630 that day. I was so angry with myself I just thought, 'Fuck it,' and frittered it all away. If I'd been sensible with my bets, I could have won thousands of pounds on the back of Doddsie's tip. Instead, I ended up with fuck all – as usual!

When I got to Dundee United, I wasn't earning as much money as I'd been on at Watford or Rangers, but I was still gambling. I tried to hide a lot of it from Caroline, but she's not daft. She knew fine well that I was losing a lot of money. Eventually, it was her who said, 'You've got a problem, you need to see someone about it.'

It was hard, but I had to admit to myself that I was struggling. That's when I decided to go to GA. For two years I was off it completely. It was difficult going to those meetings. There were people there who were gambling a tenner a day, but it was still an addiction for them. At first, I thought it was a bit embarrassing. But when I took a step back and thought about it, they didn't have that tenner to bet. They couldn't afford it. So even though I was betting hundreds of pounds at a time, their problem was every bit as bad as mine. It's an old cliché, but it wasn't nice standing up in front of people I didn't know, saying: 'I'm Charlie and I'm addicted to gambling.' Others had been off it for forty years and were still turning up. I had a lot of respect for those guys.

I told everyone in the Dundee United dressing-room; all the boys knew I was going to the meetings. Why not? It was better that it was out in the open, albeit in the confines of the changing-room.

I only started betting again when I got to Norway and played for SK Brann, and that was largely down to boredom. That's not an excuse; I just found myself with more free time, especially before Caroline and the kids came over.

Has it ever got quite as bad as it was at United? No, because now I don't have two bob to rub together. Seriously, I don't have the money to bet heavy any more. I can't do it. I still love a punt, but I know I can't afford it.

The biggest bet I ever had was £2,000 on Nick Dundee at the Cheltenham Festival in 1999. I'll never forget it. It was racing against a horse called Looks Like Trouble and was tipped as the next 'super horse'. But at the second last fence of the Royal & Sun Alliance Chase, under jockey Norman Williamson, Nick Dundee fell and broke its leg, leaving the horse fighting for his life. That allowed Looks Like Trouble to come through and win the race by a distance. I was devastated.

The following year, however, Looks Like Trouble was racing in the Gold Cup back at Cheltenham and I had £1,000 on it at 11/2. It romped in and I got £6,500 back. It was funny, because I had phoned my mate Lenny Caldwell to put the grand on it for me. I must have been at an away game and couldn't get it on. When Lenny went to collect the winnings, the bookie in Bridgeton asked if he'd accept a cheque. Typically, Lenny said, 'No fucking chance.'

The guy said, 'Are you sure you want to go out there with that kind of money?'

And Lenny said, 'Why, who the fuck is going to try and take it off me?'

That was brilliant from Lenny.

Going further back, shortly after I joined Leicester City on loan from Rangers, Caroline had left to come back up to Glasgow, so I was staying in the Stakis Hotel on my own. She wasn't coming back down for a few days, so I immediately went to the nearest bookies and put 3 x £20 doubles and a £20 treble on three different horses. All three of them won and I scooped £7,500. 'Ya fucking beauty,' I thought. I was delighted.

The next day, I went into the same bookies to have a bet on the 1999 Cup-Winners' Cup semi-final first leg between Real Mallorca and Chelsea. I put £200 on the Spanish player Dani to score first at 10/1, £200 on the 1–1 draw at 6/1 and a £100 double on both. They all came up, so I had another £7,500. I couldn't believe it. What a fucking feeling that was.

A couple of days later, Caroline came down to Old Trafford to see me playing for Leicester reserves against Manchester United reserves. I had £15,000 stashed in the boot of the car. Even in April it was a cold night, so before the game I'd given her the keys to my car in case she had to go and get an extra jacket. As soon as we got back into the car after the game, I could tell by the way she was acting that she'd seen the cash, so before she could say anything, I came clean.

I said to her, 'By the way, I won a few bob yesterday.'

She just smiled. I gave her £5,000 off it, so she wasn't complaining. That was one of the few times when my gambling brought a smile to both our faces.

Aside from the gambling, I've suffered a fair bit of heartache in my personal life over the last ten years. The deaths of my two wedding ushers – and good pals – Ricky Ward and Lenny Caldwell really hit me hard. The fact that they both took their own lives at young ages made it even more difficult to take.

Ricky was my best mate Rab's brother-in-law and he had his problems with the drink. But Ricky and I always got on great together. We were really close growing up in Castlemilk and that's why he was one of the ushers at the wedding.

Rab should really have been my best man that day, but he didn't even come to me and Caroline's big day, the bastard. He was earning good money working down in Sheffield, so we agreed he didn't have to come. Now I really regret the fact that Rab wasn't a bigger part of the wedding, because we were close pals – always have been, always will be. We'd fight like fuck, but we loved each other. Our fall-outs would last about five minutes.

I remember when we were kids, he beat me on my old Amiga console one day and I packed up the computer in a huff and stormed up to my ma's house. I got halfway up the road, stopped and thought to myself, 'What the fuck am I doing?' Rab was hanging out the window laughing at me.

Anyway, through Rab I got to know Ricky, and we spent a lot of time together. I'll never forget the day he died, because it was the day Rangers beat Celtic in the League Cup final at Hampden on 20 March 2011. He was only forty years old.

Nikica Jelavic scored the winner in extra time for Gers and I was at the game as a guest. I was actually on the pitch with the trophy before the match, along with other ex-Old Firm players. After that, I was sitting in the stand opposite the BT Stand, in the posh seats. I was sitting with Derek McInnes and my mobile phone was on silent. When I looked at it, I had around thirty missed calls and twenty text messages. Everyone was trying to get hold of me: my ma, Caroline, my brother John. Then Andy McLaren called me and told me that Ricky had hanged himself.

Immediately, I just looked at Del and said, 'I need to go, mate. Ricky has killed himself.'

Del knew Ricky himself, so he was well aware of how I would take the news. Andy picked me up at the motor showroom on Cathcart Road, just outside Hampden, with the cup final still raging on inside. I went up to Rab's ma's house and I just couldn't get my head around it.

Ricky had decided to take his own life for no apparent reason that I could see. He had become a bit of a recluse in the previous few years, but I would go up and sit with him, have a can of beer, and watch the football in his house. He rarely went out and had a few problems. All of a sudden, he'd say to me, 'Is my breath smelling? Smell my breath.' He became really paranoid and he wasn't very well. It became difficult to sit with him and I really felt for Ricky.

He wasn't into drugs, but he liked his beer. And I think that's where his main problems lay. Depression might also have been a factor. And he never ate anything. I'd watch him drink twenty cans of lager then have a bowl of soup. He'd go upstairs and be sick, before coming down to say, 'That fucking soup!'

I'd say to him, 'Are you taking the piss?' To him, it was never the beer.

When Ricky went, I was just numb with shock. A real sadness and hurt came over me. If he had died of natural causes it would have been hard to take, especially at the age of forty. But to go like that, by taking his own life, was tough to accept.

179

Ricky's missus Jamie-Lee had just given birth to his baby boy, wee Nico. As far as I knew, he was looking forward to fatherhood. But Nico was only a few months old when Ricky died, which is just tragic.

Rab was as devastated as me. The three of us were really tight, but all the boys who were around the Shop Mob when we were kids were affected by it. They were all at Ricky's funeral. It just wasn't right. He was far too young to die, and the same goes for my other mate Lenny, who had also committed suicide just four years earlier, while I played in Belgium with Lierse.

I'd known Lenny since I was a baby, as he was a friend of the family. Lenny's mum was my godmother and they stayed downstairs from us, in the same close, when I lived with my gran in Stravanan Road. He was like a brother, uncle, neighbour and best pal, all rolled into one. He was just the greatest guy you could ever meet. Lenny was older than me and he died when he was just forty-one.

He'd go round and collect rags in a van for the charities and did well for himself in that line of work. He even bought a house in Burnside, not far from me. He had a lovely family, his wife Arlene and kids Chantelle and Nicky, who I still see to this day. I haven't seen his other daughter Charlene in a while. She has moved on with her life, and good luck to her.

When I got the phone call from Caroline in July 2007 to say that Lenny had hanged himself, I just thought, 'No fucking chance.' I refused to believe it. When it began to hit home that it was true, I just broke down. To this day, we don't know the reasons for it. He wasn't a gambler, I know that. Could it have been depression? I really don't know. I'd been away for a few years in Norway and Belgium and I hadn't seen as much of him as I would have liked. I will probably never know the real reason behind it, but it hit me hard.

It was a horrible time for me and, although I'm not making excuses, it was after that that I started to drink a lot more. From that moment in Belgium, via Australia, I've hit the bevvy a lot more than I used to. I still think about Lenny and Ricky a lot.

Incredibly, in that same four-year period, I almost lost Rab as well, when he ended up on a life support machine. I was still in Belgium at that time as well. I had to deal with a few setbacks around then.

Rab was found at the foot of a set of stairs outside Bennigan's pub in Castlemilk. Was he pushed, punched or did he fall down them? We still don't really know. Even Rab can't remember, because he was out cold and at death's door.

I came back from Belgium immediately. I was given a few days off and went to the hospital every day I was back. It was a tough time for Rab's family because his wee da, Jimmy Brown, was dying of cancer around the same time. I'm convinced that his da held on to make sure his boy pulled through, because wee Jimmy was gone shortly after Rab came out of the coma.

He was in a coma for a couple of months. That was a worrying time and another real shock to the system for me. Rab's memories of the night in question are hazy, and I don't like talking to him about it. I'm just glad he's here. He suffered a cracked skull and needed an operation to have part of his brain removed. You should see the scar he has on his head as a result of it.

Rab is still as daft as a brush. Has the head injury had an effect on him? I wouldn't say so; he's just as mad as he's always been.

I really should see more of him.

181

13

END OF THE ROAD

IN modern-day football, thirty-four years of age isn't that old. Players go on for longer these days, even at the top level. If you're fit, dedicated and look after your body, you can play long into your thirties. Unfortunately, I had no such desire.

When I returned home to Scotland from Australia in 2011, I was only thirty-four. And you know what? If I'd have really pushed myself when I got back, to the level I'd been at a few years previously when I left Brann Bergen, I could easily have still played in the Scottish top flight. But I didn't. Why? Because I just couldn't be arsed any more. I know that sounds terrible, the laziest statement in the world. But it's true. That's just how I felt when I got back. I'd had my fill. In my mind, I was still good enough, but my body wasn't in the right shape to play top-level football. And I didn't have the energy to put the work in any more. My heart had gone out of the game.

I've known big Kenny Brannigan for a long time and I trained with his Queen of the South side at the Glasgow Green just to keep fit. I still enjoyed a kick-about and a bit of dressing-room banter with the boys. It was also on my doorstep. And within a month or so, Kenny had offered me a contract to play in the Scottish Championship. Queens are a decent side, so it was worth looking at, considering I'd just come back from Australia.

The money was pretty shite compared to what I was used to at previous clubs. I think it was £500 a week, but I told Kenny that I'd think about it. Because it was an easy option, I was going to sign. Anyway, it was only a deal until January, so I thought it would get me games and keep me ticking over before I decided what to do next.

But just before I went in to put pen to paper, Kenny phoned me and said he had to withdraw the offer. His chairman, Davie Rae, had pulled the plug. As far as they were concerned, I'd be taking the place of someone in the squad who'd then be getting paid for sitting in the stand, and due to the state of the finances in Scottish football, that was a step Queens couldn't afford to take. I was hardly desperate for the deal in the first place, but for it to be there and then be taken away from me, I was gutted.

That was probably the moment when I thought, 'Fuck this, I can't be bothered playing football any more.'

I was disheartened and disillusioned with the game I'd fallen in love with as a kid. The game I adored when I first broke into that Rangers first team. Suddenly it wasn't that appealing any more. As far as I could see, the game in Scotland was on its arse. There was no money floating around and, in general, it was on a downward spiral. So what was the point?

Then, out of the blue, I got a call from Jim Duffy at Clyde, who asked me how I'd feel about helping them out by playing in League Two. They were rock bottom of the league, the worst team in Scottish football. I couldn't go any lower. Was this what it had come to? But Duff is a mate, and I agreed to play a few games for him. I think I only had one proper training session with the Bully Wee on a midweek night because by that stage I was coaching and helping Andy McLaren's new company, A&M Training. I couldn't afford to be at training twice a week, missing what was now essentially my work with Andy.

In the space of five weeks, I managed to play in five games against Stranraer, Albion Rovers, Montrose and Queen's Park twice. We won just one of them – a 4–2 victory over Stranraer in my first game. I was subbed in three of the five matches late in the game and my last game in senior football came at Broadwood on Tuesday, 5 April 2011, against Montrose.

I came off the bench after an hour, replacing Willie Sawyers, and I thought I would have a hand in getting us the points when Pat Scullion scored with five minutes left. Unfortunately, Montrose equalised a minute later and it finished 1–1.

It wasn't the greatest five weeks of my career – far from it – but I did it because I love Duff and wanted to help him out if I could. People were surprised that I'd decided to drop down to that level. As I said, I still believe that if my head and body were right, I could have been playing in the top league, rather than the bottom. I was still young enough, but I just wasn't interested. And it wasn't as if I was being flooded with offers from top-flight clubs.

I might have expected the phone to ring a few times after what I'd achieved in my career as a player, but I think a few managers who might have thought about it became a bit over-protective over their jobs. I don't know why, because I wasn't interested in becoming a manager. But that's just the way I felt – I don't think they wanted an opinionated, experienced pro on board.

In any case, in my own head, I'd chucked it. I'd had enough. It was as if I'd gone full circle: I was back in Scotland again, where it had all started for me. But I didn't want to be scraping about trying to get a game, here, there and everywhere.

After what I'd experienced in Australia, in terms of the lifestyle, I also wasn't prepared to go back to training two nights a week in the pissing rain, washing my own kit and playing on shit pitches. I quickly realised that the standard of the Scottish game had deteriorated so much since I'd left Rangers back in 1999. From what I could see, it was very poor, to say the least.

In those five games for Clyde, I found myself getting caught on the ball a lot. The boys I was playing alongside were great lads; Duff had some talented kids there. But, with all due respect, I was waiting on them making certain runs during games and it just wasn't happening. I was being made to look silly by players with half of my ability. At every other club I'd played for, I'd have just made that pass, because I knew the good players I had alongside me would have made those runs naturally, without even thinking about it.

Jim probably saw it as well. He's a brilliant manager – he's now at Morton – and I speak to him and his assistant Chic Charnley often. I'm convinced they'll do well at Cappielow and get them back to where they belong.

The crowds at the Clyde games were probably less than 400 at times. That was a bit of a comedown. But, to be honest, I was never one for noticing the crowd I was playing in front of. Whether it was 50,000 at Ibrox or 300 at Broadwood, it was just a game of football to me. Nerves never really affected me on the pitch, so that didn't bother me too much at Clyde.

Nerves probably affect me more now when I play on a Saturday afternoon for Tynecastle amateurs in Glasgow. Recently, we played St Roch's in an away fixture and I took absolute dog's abuse from the side of the park. A group of Celtic fans spent an entire forty-five minutes calling me a dirty Orange bastard, which wasn't great. I ended up coming off at half-time.

Anyway, by the time I joined Clyde, I had decided I wanted to get into coaching and developing some of the city's deprived kids. When I came back to Scotland, Andy took me on board with A&M. He was going into housing schemes around Glasgow, just like Castlemilk, where we'd both grown up. It wasn't so much about coaching the kids; it was about helping them get off the street and start kicking a ball.

We had some really good boys taking part and I enjoyed working with Andy and his business partner Robert McHarg. They'd recruited other ex-pros like Robbie Winters and Scott

McLaughlin, who also got involved. I ended up working with Andy for about eighteen months, but, sadly, it all came to an end after yet another daft night out with mates.

A&M had a company van and I was in charge of it on this particular occasion. I had taken it with me on a night out – well, a house party to be more precise – and I ended up absolutely steaming drunk. I was staying with a mate, Gav Haggerty, and I fell asleep on his couch. But while I was lying sleeping, another one of the boys decided he had to go somewhere. So he took my keys and jumped in the van. He was still well over the limit and he was caught by police on Stravanan Road, in Castlemilk, with the 'stolen' van. He didn't have any insurance either. I was totally oblivious, of course. I woke up the next morning, looked out of the window and thought, 'Where the fuck is the van?'

Andy was raging, and rightly so. Robert was even more so, and we had a bit of a fall-out over it. And that was the end of me working for A&M.

Thankfully, we've kissed and made up since then and we all get on great again. Andy and I speak to each other almost every day now and we'll never fall out again. We're too good mates for that to happen.

After that, I decided to go and branch out on my own with the Charlie Miller Football Academy. By that stage, I wanted to give a bit back to the game. That's why I coach the kids now. If I see children with a talent, especially in my area, I want to coach them and do it in the right manner. My uncle Benny is fully qualified as well and he's magic with them. We want to do it properly.

I've had Robbie, José Quitongo and Boab Malcolm all working with me at different times, and I really enjoy it. We do it on a Monday and a Friday night at Toryglen Football Centre, just along from Hampden, and we'll actually run two boys' teams for season 2014/15.

The academy has been running for just over two years now and it's going well. It's not a money-making exercise. We're a commercial business, but we make very little. Sometimes, I have to pay for balls or pitches out of my own pocket, but we've got some great kids and the parents have been really supportive. I love doing it. If nothing else, it keeps me busy and out of the pub for a few hours.

I believe I can coach youngsters and make them better. It's a good feeling when you see them progressing and improving their skills.

Right now, I'm also helping John Viola with his agency. I go and watch young players and try to recruit them at an early age, so we can hopefully guide them down the right path in their careers. I'll go and watch a lot of Under-17, Under-19 and Under-20 games in Scotland and England. That's something I really enjoy because, no matter what anyone says about me, I know football and I can spot a player.

John and I get on great now. I first met JV shortly after I signed that ill-fated five-year deal at Ibrox. It was Alex Cleland who introduced him to me at Rangers and we hit it off right away. It was me who then encouraged other boys like Barry Ferguson to sign up with him. We didn't speak for a while after the return to Rangers failed to materialise in 2007 and he wasn't best pleased with my move to Lierse. We've had our ups and downs over the years, but he was best man at my wedding, and overall, he's done a good job for me.

He's a good businessman and he'd have made a good living anyway, whether I'd come along or not. I think some people have a bad perception of John, as they do with agents in general, but he's a good man and I'd trust him with my life.

Working with him has given me a new lease of life. It's been the kick up the backside that I needed. Before, there were times when I'd get really down. I get bored easily, which usually leads to more drinking and gambling. There were a lot of days when I'd be kicking about the house with nothing to do. But I've always loved watching football and that's what I'm doing now. It's especially satisfying when I know that if we recruit a player I can help him and be part of his development.

I think I can help kids a lot just by telling them my story. That tale about Walter giving me the five-year contract on terrible wages because I didn't have an agent – I must tell that to every young player's parents now. I also like spotting something in a young player that maybe others won't, and that's just because I've played the game at a high level.

We had a kid over from France recently and when John had a look he didn't fancy him. But I could see something in him. The boy started his career at Marseille and got a move to Parma before losing his way a bit. I got him into Morton with Duff and he scored two goals in a friendly match against St Mirren's Under-20 side. Duff was really impressed. His game awareness was good and he had a terrific attitude. I could see he had something. He's gone back to France now, but hopefully he'll be back in Scotland soon and we can fix him up with a club.

When I watch defenders, it's a little bit harder for me, because – as most of my managers will tell you – I'm not defensively minded. Judging players in the final third is what I'm good at.

Alan Archibald – my old Dundee United team-mate and current manager of Partick Thistle – said to me that I'll *never* sign a player up. I asked why and he said that, whoever the boy is, he'll never live up to my own standards of play. I took that as a real compliment from Archie.

I try to imagine where I'll be in ten years' time and I suppose, in a perfect world, I'll still be working closely with JV, we'll have a good stable of young players, and my wee academy will be thriving. Hopefully, the academy will produce a few gems. We won't see it now, but in ten years' time, I'm hoping the parents who I've been dealing with during that time trust me enough with their kid's future in the game. That's the plan. Obviously, Rangers, Celtic, Dundee United, Hamilton Accies and the rest will all try to steal the best kids off me. But as long as the parents have faith in me and John to look after them, we'll do well.

Some people are probably reading this and thinking, 'Why's he even bothering to work?' The general perception is that I'll have surely made enough money from a fourteen-year football career that I don't have to graft now. And maybe that should have been the case. Maybe I should be sitting in a big mansion with my feet up all day counting my cash. But nothing could be further from the truth.

The reality is that I endured a tough time financially towards the end of my time in Australia, when I had to declare myself bankrupt. JV and my friend Dave McGee got us involved in a business venture a few years ago called Cabvision. If you're sitting in the back seat of a black taxi and see a wee screen with adverts scrolling across it, that's Cabvision. I've known Dave for a long time and he got us on board in good faith. A lot of former Old Firm players, like Barry Ferguson and Chris Sutton, also got involved, but the business ran into trouble and we lost a lot of money.

The reason we bought into it was because it was supposed to provide us with a tax loophole. The idea was that it would save us cash in the long term. It was all above board and seemed like a good move at the time, but it turned into a disaster, and while I was in Australia I received a letter from HMRC in London saying I owed them £190,000. I was stunned. I thought it must be a wind-up. But it was true. There was simply no way I could pay, or afford, that amount of money. Not at that stage in my career. My only option was to declare myself bankrupt. I'm not proud of it and it's a hard thing to admit, but if I wanted to try to do the best for my wife and kids, it was a decision I had to make.

And that's why, this year, I want to get back into football in a big way. I still feel I have a lot to offer the game. I'm a good coach and, whether I like it or not, I need to go and do my SFA badges. I don't particularly agree with the system – I don't see how a badge means you suddenly know all about the game – but I have to do it and I want to do it. I think I could set a team out and coach them on a day-to-day basis. I even think I could manage a team. I'm not saying I could do it at the highest level yet, but I deserve a chance. I know how players think and what makes them tick. Any manager needs their players to play for them.

I don't want to become an assistant manager or first-team coach, because I think if you do that you have to become a grass. If you catch the players doing something or see them slacking off, you need to run to the manager. I wouldn't like that. I don't want to be a go-between. But I look at the likes of Barry Ferguson starting out at Clyde or Darren Young at Albion Rovers and I'd be willing to do something like that. Who knows if I can hack it? But I'd love the chance to prove I could do it. I know you have to earn the right, but sometimes I think I just need a break.

I have the same simple philosophy on football that I had when I broke into that Rangers team at the age of seventeen. As far as I'm concerned, coaches try to complicate football nowadays. It's become a very complex game all of a sudden. But it's not. If you have good players who are willing to play for you, you've got a chance. Any decent manager will tell you that. I think players would enjoy working under me.

But listen, I'm not holding my breath on job offers coming in. Football doesn't owe me anything. In fact, I owe the game everything. Football will still be here when I'm gone. It'll still be here when José Mourinho and Sir Alex Ferguson are gone. I just want to try to contribute something before it's too late.

I've watched the Scotland Under-16 team recently and I think the SFA's performance director, Mark Wotte, is trying to do things in the right way. But if he thinks Scotland are going to start playing the 'Dutch way', I think he'll be disappointed. The SFA are bringing kids together at Performance Schools and getting them to play in a certain way, but what happens at their clubs when they're being taught a completely different philosophy?

Anyway, I'd like to do my bit if I can. I've spent too much time doing nothing, but I've got a better outlook now. And family stuff, away from football, has taught me recently that life is too short.

Back in 2012, when my ma had been going to the doctors in pain, she was told consistently that she had piles. Eventually, she was in so much bother that she went for a second opinion at the Victoria Infirmary in Glasgow and we discovered that she has a tumour in her bowel. She was in agony. As well as that, we've since found out that she has cancer of her liver and her lung. Talk about being knocked for six. The news has hit me hard. When she told me, I just couldn't believe it. Seriously, what were the doctors doing for over a year? Not giving her the proper diagnosis could have a major impact on her in the long term.

In the same week about eight months ago, Caroline's mum, Margaret, was told she had brain cancer. You couldn't have made it up. I don't know what we've done as a family to deserve that kind of luck.

And my ma's had complications with her chemotherapy as well. When she originally went to have a PICC line put into her arm for the chemo, it was a student nurse doing it and it wasn't done right. My ma has a metal plate in her shoulder from a previous injury and, because it hadn't been fitted correctly, it caused an infection in her shoulder. So instead of getting chemo, she needed another operation on her shoulder first. It was a shame for my wee ma, she was in so much pain, and I felt helpless. She's only 56.

She's a wee fighter, though, and she is strong. So is Caroline's ma, who is battling through horrendous illness as well.

It's fair to say that 2014 has been a nightmare for the family. My ma is still going through chemo and has already had bouts of radiotherapy. The doctors are trying to manage the cancer, but she's behind schedule with the chemo and none of us are sure how she'll react to it.

My sister Susan has been magic with her up until now. She's

191

really cared for her and does the things I can't do, like wash her, and look after her that way. My brother John is still a young boy at twenty-five and has struggled to come to terms with it. He's got his own life, but I just hope he understands that, at the moment, it's all about our ma and making sure she gets better.

We're all there for her. Even though we argue at times, just like any family, we all want what's best for her. As the oldest, I'm trying to be the one who's there for her at all times. I stay with her a lot up in Castlemilk, and whenever she needs me I try to be there.

Her boyfriend, James, is also on hand to help and she's getting there. She's still young, and when something like this happens it makes you appreciate the time you've got with her. She's a funny wee woman and she still makes me laugh, despite all this adversity. I've spoken earlier on in the book about how I stayed at my gran's as a baby, but your ma is still your ma, and after everything that's happened recently it has really hit home how close I am to her. It was my gran who I lived with when I was younger, but my ma has always been there for me when I've needed her.

As far as my own family life is concerned, I see my own son and daughter every day. Caroline and I are on good terms and speak regularly. Although we've had our arguments and wee break-ups, we always end up talking again. It's because I love her.

My kids are the most important people in my life. If Jordan was any more laid-back, he'd fall over. He'll be sixteen in December 2014 and he's doing great. I've promised to take him to a Chelsea game at Stamford Bridge as a birthday present – I'll look forward to that.

He's not been without his problems. He has dyslexia and he broke his leg at a young age, meaning he's become flat-footed in later life. It was a serious incident and he could have killed himself. He fell through a glass window as a kid and ripped his leg, but it could have been a lot worse. He was helping his ma fix a bed. And before that, while I was at Watford, we got the fright of our lives with Jordan. He was only two years old and he'd stopped breathing. We rushed him to hospital and, even after he'd started breathing again, we feared he had hepatitis. The wee man has been through a lot. He's had to deal with a few obstacles in his life already, but he's getting there.

Thankfully, Demi has been fine – apart from me pulling her elbow out of its socket one day! She was play-fighting years ago with her uncle Declan and I playfully grabbed her arm and said, 'Right, that's enough, stop it.' On the way home to Bothwell, she was crying all the way in the car. She was never a 'greetin' wean', so I was a bit concerned. I was asking if she was okay and she kept complaining about a sore arm. So I took her to hospital and, sure enough, her elbow had come out of the socket. I was broken-hearted. I was gutted. I thought, 'Oh my God, what have I done?' And did I spoil my wee lassie after that day, I'll tell you!

We've now got a new addition to the family as well: wee Frankie Miller, our dog, who is a fucking nutcase.

I can't map out my kids' future, unfortunately. Of course, I want the best for them and I'll try to guide them down the right road, but they have to make their own choices in life. All I can do is be there for them if they make wrong ones along the way.

I try not to put too much pressure on them, in terms of what they want to achieve. Demi is really into her acting and drama, and I think she's clever enough to succeed. Obviously, I hope they don't make the mistakes I did at times in my career. I'll do everything I can to make sure they do well in life. Most importantly, I want them to have fun and make the most of it.

Whether I was right or wrong, that's what I always tried to do.

14

BACK HOME

I'M back in Castlemilk a lot these days. Throughout my career, I've always ended up back there. It's where I was brought up and it's where I belong.

Going back there regularly to see pals I've known since I was at Windlaw Primary School has probably been my downfall at times. I know that, and most of the managers I've worked with would say the same. But I never wanted to leave my mates behind: that's the truth of the matter. I found that side of being a footballer difficult. It was like I wanted them to share a bit of the journey with me, if that makes any sense.

I still love all my pals, the same way I did when I was back in the Shop Mob. Ironically, I don't see them as much as I'd like now because of coaching, the academy and my agency work with John Viola. But I'm still up in the old scheme nearly every day, whether it's to care for my ma, see my brother and sister or hook up with a few of my mates.

The place has changed so much over the years. There are new houses everywhere, the shops have all been renovated and the high-rise flats have been knocked down. But the people are still the same. Everyone I see from my childhood now has kids of their own, that's the scary thing. Suddenly, I'm not the eighteen-year-old running about the streets any more. Some of the young ones probably look at me now and think, 'Look at that old bastard.'

Seriously, the kids in Castlemilk nowadays don't have a clue about who I am. Even the ones who are Rangers fans can't remember me. They won't know I crossed the ball for Brian Laudrup to score the goal that sealed nine-in-a-row, but they'll go to Ibrox on a Saturday and sing about that famous achievement. It's mad, but it doesn't bother me. I've never been one to shout from the rooftops about how good I was or who I played for. That's just not me.

I suppose there won't be many of Rangers' nine-in-a-row squad who will still be walking around the area where they grew up on a daily basis. Does that make me feel bad? Not really. I've always been proud of my roots and it seems natural for me to be back in Castlemilk now.

I still get on well with the folk up there. Of course, some people will say if I'd kept away I might have got on better. But it was my choice. It was my career and my life. I lived it the way I thought was right.

EPILOGUE

SO, seventeen years after playing with Laudrup and Hateley, I'm back in that same away dressing-room at Hampden. It's Queen's Park v Clyde and we've just been hammered 4–0. I had gone to Clyde to help out a mate, Jim Duffy, who was manager. We were bottom of the league, the worst team in Scotland at the time.

No disrespect to those boys sitting next to me, but this was a totally different ball game. The ability they had was nothing like that of the team-mates I had been used to over the years. I'm the type of player who can see a pass, but I need guys around me who can make the right run and know when to make it. At Clyde it was a real struggle. I found myself being caught on the ball because I was holding on to it too long. The runs weren't being made, so I was being dispossessed. It was me who looked stupid.

There was no elation at Hampden this time: just a realisation that it was over. At thirty-five, my career was at an end. It made me think of Richard Gough's words when I was a kid at Ibrox. He told me to enjoy it while it lasts, because it flies by. I said, 'Aye, okay, big man.' But he was dead right. It's the truest saying. My career has flown by and it was over before I knew it.

By that stage at Clyde, I wasn't bothering my arse any more. Wasted talent. I know that's the perception of Charlie Miller and I can understand it. I know I could have done more. I've made

197

wrong choices in life and I wish I'd known then what I know now. Looking back, I should have done things differently off the field. I should have achieved so much more in my career. I know that now. I took my eye off the ball. I should never have left Rangers in 1999, but I wasn't as fit as I should have been. Alcohol took over. I was going out a lot and drinking too much.

Gazza's arrival didn't help, but it was my own doing. I'm not going to blame anyone else. As a teenager, I just didn't know the right way to lead my life away from football. Maybe I could have done with a bit more guidance.

I won four SPL titles, one League Cup, a Norwegian Cup and the SPFA Young Player of the Year award in 1995. But, with my ability, I should have amassed far more silverware than that. There was nothing to stop me seeing out my entire career at Rangers and breaking appearance records. I didn't do things properly – and it rankles with me. And it still angers me that I only got one Scotland cap.

I can't turn the clock back, but, in quiet moments, I sit and reflect. I have loads of regrets. I hate the fact that I didn't make the most of it and maximise the gift I had. Even now I think, 'If I'd have just done things right, I'd have been at Rangers all my days and played 700 games.'

I try not to beat myself up about it too much. You start doing daft things when you do that, but there have been times when I've got really down about it. Right now, things are tough. But I'll get through it. I always try to see light at the end of the tunnel. I have to keep going. I tell myself I played for Rangers and Scotland and won nine-in-a-row at Ibrox. That's not too bad for a wee daft boy from Castlemilk, is it?

APPENDIX

MY DREAM TEAM

CHOOSING the best eleven players I ever played alongside was a tougher task than I thought it would be, but I'm pretty confident that the side I've picked would hold its own against the very best. Naturally, the Rangers team I was involved in, which had so much success, features heavily, but I couldn't ignore others who I had the privilege of playing beside.

Some of the names might surprise you and I imagine there will be a few glaring omissions in some people's eyes. The fact that players like Richard Gough, Oleg Kuznetsov, Ian Ferguson and Andrei Kanchelskis haven't even made the bench will tell you how good it is.

But it's my team (even though I've had to pack the subs bench!) and I can genuinely say it was an honour to play with each and every one of them.

So, here goes:

4-1-3-2 FORMATION

ANDY GORAM
Goalkeeper
It had to be 'the Goalie', that's a no-brainer. He's the best shot-stopper I've ever seen. Peter Schmeichel was around at Manchester

United in the '90s but he couldn't save shots the way Andy could. At that time, Manchester United weren't any bigger than Rangers so he was right up there with Schmeichel. Sometimes the Goalie did virtually nothing, because we were battering teams, but even in those games he'd come up with a crucial save when we needed it most. In our eight-in-a-row season, Celtic only lost one game and that was against us. We won the league and it was down to one man: Andy Goram. He was frightening that year, and Tommy Burns, God rest him, once said he'd have on his grave-stone: 'Andy Goram broke my heart.' That's how good the Goalie was. I loved him when I was at Ibrox and still do now. Though he's now teetotal, when he was on the drink he was a Jekyll and Hyde character. He'd come into training as rough as guts and wouldn't train until a Thursday because of his knees. He'd be so grumpy and Ian Durrant would wind him up. But by 4 p.m. he'd have changed again, he'd be everyone's pal and asking what pub we were going to. I regard myself very fortunate to know the Goalie. He's a good friend and I have a lot of time for him.

NEIL COX
Right-back
I've opted for Neil ahead of Alex Cleland, who I played with at Rangers. Coisty christened him 'Frederick Fun Forehead' on a trip to Germany to play Borussia Dortmund, because of his huge napper, but Alex was a great guy. But I've gone for Neil, who I played with at Watford. We both signed on at Vicarage Road on the same day and immediately hit it off. We stayed in a hotel together and we became best mates down there. Along with Richard Johnson, an Australian lad, we were really close during my time at Watford. Coxy was a terrific footballer who played at the top end of the Premier League with the likes of Aston Villa, Bolton and Middlesbrough. He had a good physique, he got up and down the flank, and he could play in possession. I'm sure he was once touted for a possible England cap; that's how good he

was. Off the pitch, he was a top bloke. I got to know his family well and they were lovely people. It was difficult for me going down there and Neil knew what I was going through. He had problems too, because the gaffer Graham Taylor was a strange man with his own ideas, so Coxy was a big help to me and we're still in touch. He's the assistant manager of AFC Wimbledon and we speak regularly.

CRAIG MOORE
Centre-back
I'm convinced that if Walter Smith had played Craig at centre-back regularly, instead of shifting him to full-back and midfield, he'd have been a legendary Rangers captain. He was a top-notch player, and I could see it at an early age. He came over from Australia to Ibrox as a kid and we became pals right away. We came through the ranks at Rangers together, and what a good footballer he was. He was an athlete, good in the air, strong in the tackle – and a winner. He was solid as a rock. I only ever saw him pull out of one tackle and it was with our good friend Gary Bollan at Tannadice one day. It was Craig's first game and he was at right-back. He and Gary went for a 50–50 and there was never any holding back from meathead Bollan. He made Craig eat red ash at the side of the Tannadice pitch. Seriously, that was a big moment in Oz's development, because he realised it would be no easy ride at Rangers. Craig was quick, had great pace and rarely dived in after that. In Old Firm games, he relished battles with the likes of Henrik Larsson. He got a bit of stick from the fans at Ibrox, but he was just a young kid. I stayed with him when we both played in Australia and he's a good pal. He played in the Premier League, in the Bundesliga and at the World Cup. But, for me, he should have been Rangers skipper for many years. He has to be in my team.

ALAN McLAREN
Centre-back

This might surprise a few people, because I've picked Alan ahead of Richard Gough, who, behind John Greig, was Rangers' greatest-ever captain. But I didn't play with Goughie as often as I did with Alan. His debut was my first Old Firm game against Celtic at Hampden. Immediately, I thought, 'He's the most dour-faced, driest guy I've ever met.' I just thought he was a typical guy from Edinburgh and I didn't like him. But, honestly, as time went on, I realised that Alan is one of the nicest, funniest guys you could ever come across. What a player he was. He lacked a yard, but his sheer presence and will to win made up for that. Alan loved a tackle, and alongside Moore they'd have been a formidable defensive partnership. Goughie will probably be in everyone else's all-time Rangers team, but McLaren was something else. He always looked as if he was knackered after five minutes of every game, with that big 'Billy Beetroot' face. But people didn't realise that Alan could play. He could score goals as well – he scored against Celtic with a header at Ibrox in 1995 and I also remember a thirty-five-yard screamer against Dundee United at Tannadice. If it hadn't been for his serious knee injury, he'd have been a regular for Rangers and Scotland for years.

ERLEND HANSTVEIT
Left-back

This was a tough one, because Davie Robertson at Rangers was a brilliant left-back and could easily have played in this side. Arthur Numan is another one who deserves a mention. But I've gone with Erlend, who I played with at Brann Bergen. I had to put Erlend in after all the bad things I did to him in Norway! Honestly, I used to rip up his clothes every day, put holes in all his socks – you name it, I did it to him. But he took it all in great spirit. He was the most laid-back guy I've ever met in my life, but he was a really good footballer. I think if Erlend had a yard more pace, he'd have been a real top player. He actually had a trial at Celtic a few years ago and it didn't quite happen for him. But I loved playing alongside him, and while I was at Brann he kept Christian Kalvenes, who went on to play for Dundee United and Burnley, out of the team. He went on to win caps for Norway and he's still at Brann now – he's played more than 200 games for the club. I got on well with Erlend and his work rate was incredible. He'd love playing in this side.

BARRY FERGUSON
Defensive midfield
It may surprise some people, but I felt I had to have Barry in the side as my anchorman – even though I only really had six months with him at Rangers. I just loved him in that position, sitting in front of the back four. In that role, along with Claude Makélélé when he was at Chelsea, Barry is the best I've seen in Britain. He's the most gifted I've ever played with, in terms of how he could control a game single-handedly. That's such a difficult thing to do, but Barry did it with ease and he's still doing it now. With him, Durranty and Gazza in the same side, they'd probably have to have a ball each – that was how much they wanted to get on it. Dick Advocaat made him Rangers captain and built his team around him. He gave Barry the confidence to go on and become a great player for the club. It annoyed me when he left Ibrox for Blackburn Rovers, because he could have played at an Arsenal or a Liverpool. As an all-round footballer, he was fantastic.

IAN DURRANT
Right midfield
Even in training, Durranty was just special. He'd take us all out to get drunk in the afternoons, and the next day we'd all be hungover but he could run like mad. He did it deliberately so he could take the mickey out of us on the training pitch. He was brilliant with both feet, he was a direct runner who always wanted

to score goals, and he had a great knack of arriving late in the box to get on the end of things. His passing was superb, he could ping it about all day, and just to play with the wee man was a real privilege for me. What a player he was – and that was me playing with him after his long-term injury. Durranty came back from one of the most horrendous knee injuries I've ever come across in my career. No player I've ever known has suffered more than he has. For that alone, he deserves to be in the team, and he'd have thrived in this midfield quartet.

PAUL GASCOIGNE
Central midfield
Who else could it be? The main man. The maniac. The fact he has a whole chapter dedicated to him in this book tells you how I feel about Gazza. As a player? He was just a special, unique talent who had absolutely everything. Imagine him and Durrant playing together at their peak: they'd have been scarily good. The first time I encountered Gazza, I just thought he was a cheeky bastard. Because he'd 'lend' you the ball when you were in a poor position, but he'd give you it because he knew you'd have to give him it straight back because you had two or three men around you. He was always on the move and so intelligent. Say what you like about his daftness off the pitch, but trust me, Gazza was a clever human being. He had an unbelievable football brain and that made him a phenomenal player who instantly became a hero in the eyes of the Rangers fans. Like Laudrup, he'd win games on his own and his ability was ridiculous at times.

BRIAN LAUDRUP
Left midfield
Brian was just an immense guy – and what a footballer he was. He was strong and powerful and he had an unbelievable turn of pace over the first few yards. He won games on his own for Rangers during his time at the club. We had our backs to the wall in certain games

and the Goalie would save us at one end, then Brian would stick the ball in the net at the other. I'll never forget one day at East End Park against Dunfermline. Their assistant manager, Dick Campbell, was on the touchline shouting at their right-back who was up against Brian. He had turned the boy inside out and Dick shouted, 'Do you not watch *Sportscene*, he does that turn every time!'

The guy's response was, 'Well, you try and get the fucking ball off him then!'

He was just superb. For someone at 6 ft, his touch was amazing. His ability was incredible and he was quite rightly named in the greatest-ever Rangers team. He was also a good-looking guy whose hair never moved! Seriously, Brian was and still is a lovely guy who I got on well with. He loved life in Scotland after he arrived from AC Milan.

MARK HATELEY
Striker
I played with Mark for two years at Ibrox and he was just awesome, absolutely exceptional. He was a brute up front at his peak. When he was on his game, he frightened the life out of defenders. Mark had a cracking left foot and when it fell to his right he just passed it into the net. Everyone knows about his heading ability. He was brilliant in the air and I loved playing off him – he was a big help to me as a young boy breaking into the team. The number of goals he scored that were bullet headers was incredible. He must have been a nightmare to play against, because he had such an intimidating presence on the pitch. However, I was desperate for Walter to drop him one day because we used to all sit with our suits on in the dressing-room waiting for the team to be read out. But such was Mark's confidence, he just used to get stripped and put his gear on. Just one day, I'd have loved Walter to say, 'You're on the bench big man' – just to see his face. It would have been hilarious, but he was so good that that never happened to him. He picked himself.

ALLY McCOIST
Striker
What more can you say about Coisty as a striker? He'd go to head a ball off one side of his head and it would go in off the other. If he fell in the Clyde, he'd come out with a salmon in his pocket. When I watched him as a kid, I just thought he was a good player. But when I actually trained with him for the first time, I thought, 'What a finisher this guy is.' Coisty became a better player as he got older and he was just so clever in and around the box. He became a better link-up player, and he got wise with age and experience. You'd watch him with a defender and he'd bump them, then in a split second he was in to score. He scored one-inch goals, twenty-yard goals, free kicks, penalties – every type you could think of, Coisty scored them. People forget about the quality of his finishing, but he wasn't just a poacher – even if he was jammy into the bargain! He deserves everything he's got out of the game because he worked hard for it. As a guy, he's one of the funniest I've ever come across and we had some great times together at Rangers.

SUBS
DEREK McINNES
I had to put my pal in, because I love him to bits. We had a great time together at Rangers, and what an attitude he had. He's definitely a better manager than he was a player, though.

STUART McCALL
He was a tiger in the middle of the park and a big help to me when I first got into the Rangers team. Stuarty loved a tackle and was a groundsman's nightmare. A good man.

RICHARD JOHNSON
Richard was an Aussie midfielder who helped me a lot when I was going through a tough time at Watford and a really cultured

footballer who played for the Socceroos. A knee injury hampered his career.

MATT McKAY
It didn't work out for Matty when I helped bring him to Rangers, but I'm adamant that he's a superb midfield player. He did my running for me at Brisbane Roar and is a born winner.

MARTIN ANDRESEN
Martin was captain of Norway at one stage and played in the Premier League with Blackburn Rovers. He's a real top player who I enjoyed linking up with at Brann Bergen.

RAYMOND VISFIG
Raymond played on the left side and was a hugely talented player for Brann. He had loads of flair out wide and could have played at a much higher level. Unfortunately, he was even lazier than me!

JÖRG ALBERTZ
The Hammer was a great lad and had a cannon for a left foot. He scored some wonderful goals for Rangers and we're still friends now, despite the odd difference of opinion!

WALTER SMITH
Manager
Most people think Walter would have been an automatic choice for me, but Frank Farina ran him close. My Australian gaffer was the best man-manager I had, in terms of how he let you go out and express yourself on the pitch. But it has to be Walter here. We had a love-hate relationship and I know I wasn't the most well-behaved boy in the dressing-room. What can I say – he gave me my big chance at Rangers and I'll be forever grateful to him for that. Walter knew how good a dressing-room he had and he

let us get on with it. Maybe he was a bit harder on me than others, but he was probably trying to help me and I didn't realise it at the time. His success, alongside Archie Knox, was phenomenal and no one can argue with what he achieved at Ibrox during those nine-in-a-row years.